Herbert Puchta  Günter Gerngross  Peter Lewis-Jones

# Super Minds

## American English

### Student's Book 5

# Map of the book

## The science class (pages 4–9)

| Vocabulary | Grammar | Story and value | Thinking skills |
|---|---|---|---|
| Experiments | *Nobody had a test.* *Phoebe didn't have music.* *Patrick loved all three subjects.* *What did you do at school today?* | *The explosion* Following instructions carefully | Problem solving |

▷ **Song:** The Time Travelers  ▷ **Phonics:** Rhyming words

## 1 Disaster! (pages 10–21)

| Vocabulary | Grammar | Story and value | Skills | Thinking skills | English for school |
|---|---|---|---|---|---|
| Around Pompeii | *When the earthquake happened, Mr. Harmer and his sons were playing soccer.* *While Mom was working in the yard, the dog was eating her socks.* | *A narrow escape* Helping people in danger | Reading and speaking Listening and writing | Understanding text coherence | **Geography:** Volcanoes |

▷ **Song:** Danger!  ▷ **Phonics:** final e  ▷ **Communication**  ▷ **Review:** My portfolio

## 2 In the rain forest (pages 22–33)

| Vocabulary | Grammar | Story and value | Skills | Thinking skills | English for school |
|---|---|---|---|---|---|
| Rain forest life | *one hundred – five million* *You have to wear a shirt.* *Do I have to bring any food?* *You don't have to bring any food.* | *The present* Respecting other cultures | Listening, writing, and speaking Reading and speaking | Scanning a text for time references Applying world knowledge | **Environmental studies:** The rain forest |

▷ **Functional language dialog**  ▷ **Creativity**  ▷ **Review:** My portfolio

## 3 The rock 'n' roll show (pages 34–45)

| Vocabulary | Grammar | Story | Skills and value | Thinking skills | English for school |
|---|---|---|---|---|---|
| At a rock concert | *I'm going to see the Suzy Slick show.* *Are you going to buy the new Suzy Slick album?* *It's five past five.* | *Elvis* | Listening and speaking Reading Not giving up | Applying linguistic knowledge Identifying patterns | **Music:** Rhythm |

▷ **Song:** Come rock with me  ▷ **Phonics:** <u>r</u>ock or <u>r</u>oll  ▷ **Communication**  ▷ **Review:** My portfolio

## 4 Space restaurant (pages 46–57)

| Vocabulary | Grammar | Story | Skills | Thinking skills | English for school and value |
|---|---|---|---|---|---|
| In a restaurant | *The 2nd (second) of May is a Tuesday.* *If you put honey in your tea, it becomes sweet.* | *The birthday meal* | Reading and speaking Writing and listening | Logical thinking Putting a monetary value on things Categorizing | **Biology:** Healthy food Eating healthily |

▷ **Functional language dialog**  ▷ **Creativity**  ▷ **Review:** My portfolio

## 5  The Wild West (pages 58–69)

| Vocabulary | Grammar | Story | Skills and value | Thinking skills | English for school |
|---|---|---|---|---|---|
| Wild West | The saddle's made of leather. It's used for riding horses. The baby's hat. The babies' hats. | The bank robbery | Reading Listening, writing, and speaking Understanding and learning about other cultures | Showing an understanding of character and situation | **Geography:** Gold |

▶ **Song:** The meanest robber in town  ▶ **Phonics:** double consonants  ▶ **Communication**  ▶ **Review:** My portfolio

## 6  In Istanbul (pages 70–81)

| Vocabulary | Grammar | Story and value | Skills | Thinking skills | English for school |
|---|---|---|---|---|---|
| Souvenirs | You shouldn't go out without a hat. You should always be careful when crossing the road. Could I try on that T-shirt over there? Do you mind if I close the door? | Lost in the city Showing interest in the wider world | Listening, reading, and writing Listening, speaking, and writing | Orientation in space | **Geography:** Town planning |

▶ **Functional language dialog**  ▶ **Creativity**  ▶ **Review:** My portfolio

## 7  The story teller (pages 82–93)

| Vocabulary | Grammar | Story | Skills and value | Thinking skills | English for school |
|---|---|---|---|---|---|
| Shakespeare's Globe | I'll ask my sister to give us a bracelet. She's just cut her finger. | Helping Shakespeare | Listening, reading, and speaking Reading Being honest | Applying knowledge Creative thinking | **Literature:** Poetry |

▶ **Song:** You'll never buy me rings  ▶ **Phonics:** silent e  ▶ **Communication**  ▶ **Review:** My portfolio

## 8  Museum of the future (pages 94–105)

| Vocabulary | Grammar | Story and value | Skills | Thinking skills | English for school |
|---|---|---|---|---|---|
| Jobs | If you're tired, it'll do your homework. Let's go to the museum. But what if it's closed? | The trouble with Orange-head XR-97 Helping people | Speaking, listening, reading, and writing Speaking, reading, and writing | Lateral thinking Applying world knowledge | **Math:** Fractions |

▶ **Functional language dialog**  ▶ **Creativity**  ▶ **Review:** My portfolio

## 9  Mystery at sea (pages 106–117)

| Vocabulary | Grammar | Story | Skills | Thinking skills | English for school and value |
|---|---|---|---|---|---|
| On board | I've already done my math homework. He hasn't visited Argentina yet. Have you cleaned your room yet? | The Mary Celeste | Reading and speaking Listening and writing | Imaginative interpretation of a text Applying world knowledge | **Geography:** Oceans and seas Learning about the environment |

▶ **Song:** Drop the anchor  ▶ **Phonics:** look and put  ▶ **Communication**  ▶ **Review:** My portfolio

**Grammar focus:** pages 118–127

# The science class

Alex, Phoebe, and Patrick are good friends. They all go to the same school. Today they are in science class. They are having problems doing an experiment. Their teacher, Mr. Davis, isn't very happy.

1. shelf
2. goggles
3. instructions
4. apron
5. explosion
6. bubbles
7. test tube
8. liquid
9. gloves
10. powder

**1**  Listen and say the words. Check with your partner.

**2** CD1 03 **Read, listen, and answer the questions.**

1. How many spoonfuls of blue powder did Patrick use?
2. How many spoonfuls of blue powder did the instructions ask for?
3. What does Mr. Davis ask Patrick to put on?
4. What does Mr. Davis say about safety in the classroom?

**3** **Choose a word. Draw it for your partner to guess.**

**1** **Think!** **Read the clues and check (✓) the subjects.**

Alex, Patrick, and Phoebe are sometimes in different classes. What classes did they have yesterday afternoon?

Phoebe only had two classes.

Alex, Phoebe, and Patrick watched a movie.

|  | Music | History | Science |
|---|---|---|---|
| Alex |  |  |  |
| Patrick |  |  |  |
| Phoebe |  |  |  |

Phoebe didn't sing a song and didn't listen to any music.

The movie was about life in Ancient Rome.

Patrick loved all three subjects.

Alex only had one subject.

**2**  **CD 1 04** **Grammar focus** **Listen and say the sentences.**

One of the children **had** three subjects.
Nobody **had** a test.
Alex, Phoebe, and Patrick **watched** a movie.
Phoebe **didn't have** music.
Patrick **loved** all three subjects.

**3** **Imagine that yesterday was your perfect day. Describe it to your partner.**

Yesterday was great. I got up at ten o'clock. I ate a candy bar for breakfast, and I watched three Spiderman movies on TV. Then I ...

**1** Listen and write the names. Then sing the song.

1   This person is not very patient. _____

2   This person went after Phoebe. _____

3   This person is Phoebe's best friend. _____

4   This person is never early. _____

5   These people can go to the past and the future. _____

Phoebe was the first one,
She didn't want to wait.
Now she's lost in time because
She stepped into that gate.

Alex followed Phoebe
Because best friends don't wait.
Now he's lost in time because
He stepped into that gate.

Patrick was the last one,
But then, he's always late.
Now he's lost in time because
He stepped into that gate.

The Time Travelers,
They're lost in time,
They'll never come back
If they cross that line.

The Time Travelers,
Traveling so fast,
The past is the present,
And the future is the past.

 **2** Listen and say the dialog.

**Sue**   Do you want to go through the gate, too?

**Ben**   Let's follow the friends till the story ends!

Phonics focus: rhyming words

**1** **Read and choose the correct face for each of the children.**

1

 a
 b
 c

| Mom | Did you have a good day at school today, Alex? |
| Alex | It was OK. |
| Mom | Just OK? |
| Alex | Yes. It was just a normal day. Nothing special. |

2

 a
 b
 c

| Dad | How was school today, Patrick? |
| Patrick | It was the worst day ever. |
| Dad | Why was it so bad? |
| Patrick | Our soccer team lost 6–0, and I was the goalkeeper. |

3

 a
 b
 c

| Mom | What did you do at school today, Phoebe? |
| Phoebe | We talked about the geography project, and guess what? |
| Mom | What? |
| Phoebe | I'm doing a project on Mexico! I'm so excited. |

**2**   **Grammar focus** **Listen and say the questions.**

**What did** you do at school today?
**Did** you **have** a good time?
**How was** school today?
**Why was** it a bad day?

**3** **Imagine that yesterday was the worst day ever. Ask your partner about it.**

What time did you get up?

I woke up at six o'clock. My baby sister cried so loudly.

**1** **Work in pairs. Look at the pictures and the title of the story.**

a    Write down words that come to your mind.

b    Try and make a story out of the words.

**2** CD 1 11    **Read and listen to the story to find out if it is similar to or different from your story.**

# THE EXPLOSION

Alex read aloud the instructions for the next experiment. "Add one spoonful of yellow powder to the blue liquid," he read. Phoebe followed the instruction. "It's turned green!" she said. Patrick was not very impressed. "Yellow and blue make green," he said. "Everyone knows that!" "Wait!" said Alex. "There are more instructions. Now take some of the liquid and drop it on the brick." Phoebe did this, and the brick turned purple. "Wow!" she said. "That's amazing!" "It's boring," said Patrick. "Can we do the next experiment?"

For the next experiment, Patrick read, and Alex followed his instructions. He put two spoonfuls of white powder and one spoonful of red powder into a test tube. Then he added some pink liquid. It quickly turned orange. "Now pour some of the orange liquid onto the brick," said Patrick. Alex did this, and amazingly the brick started to get bigger. "Wow!" said Alex. "That's fantastic!" Mr. Davis came to look at their experiment. "Good work," he said, "but don't forget to read the instructions carefully for your next experiment." "That wasn't very interesting," said Patrick. "Let's do the next one."

"OK, it's your turn to do it," said Phoebe. She read the instructions. "OK, we need some blue powder, some green powder, some orange powder, and some green liquid." While Patrick was getting all the things together, he knocked over a small cup of water. The water went all over the instructions. "Careful, Patrick!" said Phoebe. "Oh, no! There's water on the instructions now, and I can't read a thing." "Let's ask Mr. Davis for some more instructions," said Alex. "Don't be silly," said Patrick. "I have everything here. We just need to mix it together and put it on the brick."

"But we don't know how many spoonfuls of each powder we need," said Alex. "Don't worry," said Patrick, "let's experiment." Patrick poured all the blue powder into the orange and green powder. Then he added all the green liquid. Suddenly there was a big explosion and a bright red flash. "Wow!" said Patrick. "Now that *was* amazing. I think I added a little too much liquid," he laughed. Alex and Phoebe didn't think it was funny.

"What's that?" said Alex. He was pointing to a strange, glowing light. It was yellow, and it looked like a kind of gate. "It's really strange!" said Phoebe. The children walked toward the light and stepped into it. They were gone in a flash.

**3** **Read and answer the questions.**

Which experiment (1, 2, or 3) ...

1 does Alex do?
2 does Phoebe read the instructions for?
3 makes a yellow light?
4 changes the color of the brick?
5 makes the brick bigger?
6 goes wrong?

**4** **What do you need for each experiment? Write 1st, 2nd, or 3rd next to the pictures.**

# 1 Disaster!

Pompeii was a city of 20,000 people in the south of Italy 2,000 years ago. It was a very modern city. Lots of the houses had running water. There was a busy marketplace and a theater, and there were lots of stores. The storekeepers sold things that came on big ships from different countries around the world. The city was full of beautiful works of art.

1. smoke
2. volcano
3. temple
4. columns
5. fountain
6. theater
7. horse and cart
8. servant
9. statue
10. vase

**1** CD 1 12 **Listen and say the words. Check with your partner.**

**2** CD 1 13 **Read, listen, and complete the sentences.**

1. The gate takes the children into the _____.
2. Phoebe likes the gardens with the _____ and the _____.
3. There are no cars, only _____ and _____.
4. The mountain is not a mountain. It's a _____.

**3** **Choose a word. Mime it for your partner to guess.**

Look! Can you guess the word?

I'm not sure ... Is it ... ?

**1** Read the newspaper text and write the names under the pictures. There is one extra picture.

## Earthquake shakes London

At 5:37 p.m. yesterday many Londoners suddenly felt the earth shake. We talked to some of them this morning to hear their stories.

"My sons and I were playing soccer," said Ken Harmer from Wimbledon. "We didn't feel much, and we weren't worried." "I was in the living room," said his wife, Claire. "I was reading – it was strange!" Their neighbor Caroline was sleeping when it happened. "It was terrible. I was so scared!" she said. Another man, Mr. Singh, told us, "When I felt the earthquake, I was standing on the balcony of our apartment. It's on the 27th floor. I didn't know what to do, so I sat down!"

**2** CD 1 14 Grammar focus **Listen and say the sentences.**

> When the earthquake happened:
> ... Mr. Harmer and his sons **were playing** soccer.
> ... his wife **was reading** in the living room.
> ... their neighbor **was sleeping**.

**3** Ask and answer.

What were you doing yesterday at five o'clock?

I was ...

**1** CD 1 15 **Listen and correct the mistakes.**
**Then sing the song.**

I was ~~sleeping~~ in the gardens, (1)_____
When the ground began to shake,
A vase fell in the fountain, (2)_____
The fountain fell in the lake.
I ran inside the store, (3)_____
And I thought, "No, this is it!"
Yeah, I was feeling pretty angry when ... (4)_____
The earthquake hit.

Danger. Danger. Danger, everywhere!
Life is full of danger,
You'd better take care!

I was walking in the city, (5)_____
When the day turned really gray.
I looked up at the clouds (6)_____
And I knew I couldn't stay.
There was rain in the clouds, (7)_____
There was smoke and thunder, too.
I was feeling pretty happy when the ... (8)_____
Volcano blew.

**All about music: Punk Rock**

The first punk bands came from the U.S.A. and U.K. in the mid-1970s. Bands like The Ramones and The Clash wanted to change music forever. Their songs were fast, short, and often very angry. Punk was about fashion, too – scruffy torn clothes, amazing hair styles, and lots of safety pins.

**What I think**
▶ It's great.
⏸ It's OK.
✗ I don't really like it.

**2** CD 1 17 **Listen and say the dialog.**

**Grandma** Your haircut is cute, Stan!
**Stan** I like your cap and cape, Grandma!

**1** **Read Christopher's email to his friend. Some of the words were accidentally deleted. Look at the pictures and correct the email.**

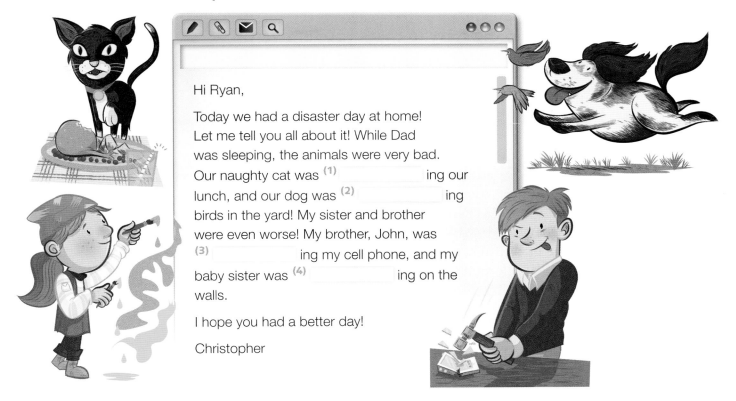

Hi Ryan,

Today we had a disaster day at home! Let me tell you all about it! While Dad was sleeping, the animals were very bad. Our naughty cat was <sup>(1)</sup> _____ ing our lunch, and our dog was <sup>(2)</sup> _____ ing birds in the yard! My sister and brother were even worse! My brother, John, was <sup>(3)</sup> _____ ing my cell phone, and my baby sister was <sup>(4)</sup> _____ ing on the walls.

I hope you had a better day!

Christopher

**2** CD1 20 **Grammar focus** **Listen and say the sentences.**

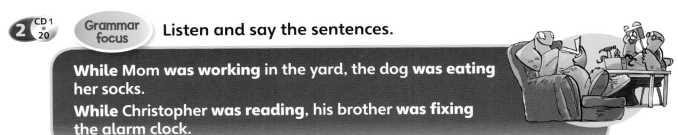

**While** Mom **was working** in the yard, the dog **was eating** her socks.
**While** Christopher **was reading**, his brother **was fixing** the alarm clock.

**3** **Play the *Wishidishing* game with a partner. Say a sentence. Your partner has to guess.**

On Sunday afternoon while I was playing computer games, my mom was *wishidishing*.

No, she wasn't.

No.

Yes, she was!

While you were playing computer games, your mom was reading.

Was she sleeping?

Was she listening to music?

**1** Go through the text quickly and find answers to the questions.

a Where are the kids?    b What year is it?

**2** Read and listen to the story to check your answers.

# A narrow escape

Phoebe started running down the stone stairs. "Hey, wait!" Alex shouted. "Where are you going?" "Hurry up! Follow me!" Phoebe shouted. "Why?" Alex and Patrick didn't understand what was happening. Phoebe was running through the city in the direction of the hills. Alex and Patrick followed her. They ran past the houses and the beautiful temples with their statues and columns, but Alex and Patrick didn't have time to look at any of that. They followed Phoebe up a hill outside the city.

When Phoebe reached the top of the hill, she sat down, and the boys sat down next to her.

"I don't understand!" said Patrick. "What are we doing here?" Phoebe waited for her breathing to slow down. Then she began to speak. She looked worried. "This city is Pompeii. We learned about it in history. That volcano over there is going to erupt, and we're in danger!" "But how do you know it's going to erupt now?" asked Alex.

Suddenly there was a loud noise like thunder. The three friends looked up at the volcano. They were scared by what they saw. There was a lot of dark, gray smoke. "I was right," said Phoebe. "We have to go and tell the people who live in Pompeii." "But are you certain it's going to erupt?" asked Alex. "Look!" said Phoebe. "Animals often run away from natural disasters. We learned that at school. Now come on! The people are in danger."

Back in the city the children tried to tell everyone about the volcano, but the people didn't understand what they were saying, so they were not worried. Suddenly there was another loud explosion.

"Look!" shouted Phoebe. "It's too late! It's erupting." Everybody was very scared. The sky got really dark, and smoke filled the air. Stones flew from the volcano and landed in the city. People started to run away shouting for help. The children didn't know what to do. Suddenly Alex saw a yellow light through the smoke. "What's that? Look!" Phoebe and Patrick saw it, too.

"I know what that is. It's the gate that brought us here!" Phoebe shouted. "Let's go through it." "The gate?" Patrick didn't understand. "Yes," said Phoebe. "Remember the lab? The yellow glow – the gate to the past? Maybe it'll take us back to our time. Let's run, or we'll all die! It's our only chance!" The children ran as fast as they could to the light and jumped. They were gone in a flash!

On August 29 in AD 79, Vesuvius erupted and destroyed the city of Pompeii. The volcano threw smoke and stones more than 30 kilometers high into the air. Within minutes, the stones, lava, and ashes covered the whole city. Almost 20,000 people died.

**3** **Put the sentences in the correct order.**

☐ They tried to warn people.　　☐ Phoebe told the boys about Pompeii.

☐ They heard a loud noise.　　☐ Suddenly they saw a bright light!

☐ The children ran up a hill.

**4** **Think!** **Work in pairs. Read the sentences. Check the text and then replace the underlined words with more specific information.**

1 They often run away from natural disasters.　　3 ... they were not worried.

2 They're in danger.　　4 They ran as fast as they could ...

Let's find "natural disasters" in the text.

Here it is. Let's look. OK. It says ...

**1** **Read the text from a news website. Write *t* (true) or *f* (false).**

1 Natural disasters can happen all over the world. ☐

2 Scientists can stop weather disasters from happening. ☐

3 Scientists can warn us about volcanoes, but not about earthquakes. ☐

4 Floods often cause lots of damage. ☐

5 Weather and people can cause forest fires. ☐

flood

hurricane

earthquake

forest fire

avalanche

# How much do you know about natural disasters?

**MAKE SURE YOU'RE DISASTER SMART – THE MORE YOU KNOW, THE BETTER.**

■ Natural disasters happen all over the world. We cannot stop them from happening.

■ The weather causes some disasters, like thunderstorms, floods, hurricanes, and avalanches. Scientists often know when weather disasters will happen.

■ Scientists have special equipment to watch volcanoes and earthquakes, but it's hard to know when these disasters will happen. That is why volcanoes and earthquakes cause a lot of damage.

■ Statistics show that floods are the most expensive natural disasters.

■ Forest fires can happen because of lightning, but also because people are not careful and make a fire in very dry places.

■ Earthquakes are the deadliest of all natural disasters because they kill more people each year than any other disaster.

■ It's a good idea to find out what kinds of disasters can happen where you live.

■ When people choose a place to live, they should think about what disasters can happen. For example, people shouldn't build houses close to rivers if there is a danger of floods.

**2** **Work in groups of four. Think of a disaster you heard about / read about / watched on TV or experienced yourself. Tell your classmates about it.**

A terrible flood happened in …

**1** CD 1 22 **Listen to a radio show about a natural disaster and answer the questions.**

1 When did the flood in New Orleans happen?

2 What have people lost?

3 What did people need?

4 How many people died?

**2** CD 1 23 **Listen again and match the sentence halves.**

1 The Red Cross and the Red Crescent

2 A few years ago, there was a terrible

3 It was called Katrina, and it

4 Thousands of people lost their families,

5 People didn't have clean water, they

6 The helpers worked day and night for

a killed lots of people.

b their homes, and their jobs.

c are one organization with two names.

d hurricane in the city of New Orleans.

e many weeks to help the people of New Orleans.

f had no food, and they needed medical help.

**3** **Think of a natural disaster (real or imaginary). Use the questions to write a short text.**

• What was the disaster?

• Where did it happen?

• When did it happen?

• What were you doing when it happened?

• What damage was there? (Houses broken? People dead?)

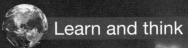 **Learn and think**

# Volcanoes

**1** **Look at the pictures. Which of them shows a volcano? What do volcanoes look like?**

Volcanoes are …

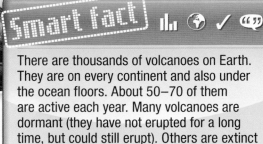

**2** **Read the article to find out how volcanoes erupt. Write the words on the picture.**

ash clouds   magma chambers   crater   lava

## Smart fact

There are thousands of volcanoes on Earth. They are on every continent and also under the ocean floors. About 50–70 of them are active each year. Many volcanoes are dormant (they have not erupted for a long time, but could still erupt). Others are extinct (they have not been active for thousands of years, and they will not erupt again).

## Fire from inside Earth

Imagine a bottle of cola. What happens when you shake the bottle and open it? The drink will explode out of the bottle. This is because the bubbles in the drink are made of gas. When you shake the bottle, there is more pressure. When you open the bottle, the gas comes out very fast.

The same thing happens when a volcano *erupts*. Earth is very hot under the surface. It's so hot that the rock is liquid. This liquid rock is called magma. The temperature of magma is very high, between 700°C and 1,300°C. Magma forms big caves inside Earth. They are called chambers. When pieces of rock fall into the magma, they make gas. When the pressure of the gas is very high, the gas and the magma come up through a hole. The hole is called a crater. We often see ash clouds coming out from the crater before an eruption.

When magma comes out of the crater, it's called lava. When lava gets cold, it becomes stone.

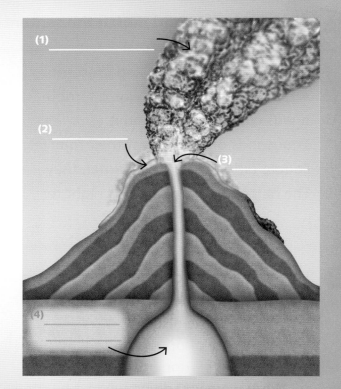

**1** (Project) **Make your own volcano. Look, read, and order the pictures.**

**You need:**
- one sheet of thin cardboard
- one sheet of thick cardboard
- one empty bottle, not too big
- some paints for decoration
- a roll of scotch tape
- a few sheets of newspaper

1 Put the bottle upside down on the thin cardboard and draw a circle around it.

2 Cut out the circle.

3 Fold the cardboard to form a cone. Put some tape on it.

4 Cut the cone so it is straight and the same height as the bottle. Put the bottle inside. Use the scotch tape to fix the mouth of the bottle to the cardboard.

5 Turn the cone upside down, with the bottle in the middle. Use crumpled newspaper to fill the cone.

6 Put the cone on the thick cardboard. Paint your volcano.

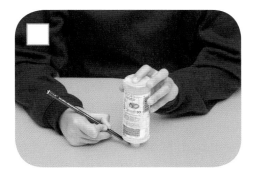

**2** **Now make your volcano erupt.**

**You need:**
- water
- two big spoonfuls of baking soda
- four or five drops of detergent
- vinegar

1 Take the bottle out of the volcano.

2 Fill the bottle almost full with water.

3 Put four or five drops of detergent into the water.

4 Add two big spoonfuls of baking soda.

5 Put the bottle back in the volcano.

6 Pour some vinegar into the bottle.

7 Watch the eruption!

# A mini-talk

**1** CD 1 25 **Listen to a group presentation about a tornado. Put the pictures in order.**

## Find out about it

- Choose a disaster and find out more about it. Possible topics are: a flood, a mudslide, an avalanche, an earthquake, the eruption of a volcano, a fire, or a tsunami.
- Use books and magazines.
- Talk to people in your family.
- Go online and see what you can find on the Internet.

## Prepare it

- Work in groups of four.
- Find out some important facts about the disaster. Make notes on a big sheet of paper.
- Find four different pictures and print them out. Make sure the pictures are big enough for your classmates to see from a distance.
- Write your talk. Each of you should write three or four sentences about your picture. Then show it to your teacher to help you with the language.
- Correct the text. Read it often enough so that you know what you are going to say.

**2** CD 1 26 **Listen again and answer the questions.**

1 What is a tornado?
2 What happened to Joplin, Missouri, in the U.S.A.?

## Present it

- Tell your classmates about your topic.
- Point to your pictures while you are talking to make it more interesting.

 **Tips for presenters**

You should give a talk, not just read aloud your text. That's why you should prepare your presentation well, so you know what you are going to say. When you talk, look at your classmates. This makes your talk more interesting.

A tornado is a very strong wind.

The tornado in Joplin was in 2011.

It destroyed lots of buildings.

# Filling in a form

**1** Start a new portfolio for this year. Write about yourself in your profile.

### My portfolio

My name:
Antulio Martinez

My class:
6e

My teacher's name:
Mrs. Wilkins

What my friends like about me:
I am funny and good at singing.

What I did during my summer vacation:
I went to Lake Louise Summer Camp.

My favorite topics:
My favorite topics are rain forests and geography!

What I like best about my English classes:
I like singing songs in English best!

**2** During his summer vacation, Antulio went to a summer camp. Read the form and answer the questions below.

## Lake Louise Summer Camp

PLEASE WRITE IN CAPITAL LETTERS

| | |
|---|---|
| Last name: | MARTINEZ |
| First name: | ANTULIO |
| Nationality: | MEXICAN |
| Sex: | ✓ M ☐ F |
| Date of birth: | AUGUST 5, 2002 |
| Place of birth: | MEXICO CITY |
| Passport no: | TR 84902658 |
| Home address (street): | 1702, CALLE SAN JOSE |
| Town/Country: | BUENA VISTA, MEXICO |
| Zip code: | 37604 |
| Email: | speedy@mail.mex |

1 What's his first name?

2 What's his last name?

3 When was he born?

4 What's his home address?

5 What country is he from?

6 What's his email address?

### Tips for writers

When you need to fill in a form, make sure you understand what you have to write. Sometimes you can guess what the words mean, but always check with someone just to make sure.

**3** In pairs, ask and answer questions. Then make a form for your partner. Check their answers.

# 2 In the rain forest

The Amazon rain forest is very large. It's called the Amazon because of the river that runs through it. The rain forest crosses nine South American countries: Brazil, Colombia, Peru, Venezuela, Ecuador, Bolivia, Guyana, French Guiana, and Suriname. The biggest part of the Amazon rain forest is in Brazil.

1 creeper
2 beak
3 toucan
4 sloth
5 branch
6 anaconda
7 pool
8 jaguar
9 anteater

**1** CD 1 27   Listen and say the words. Check with your partner.

**2** CD 1 28   **Read, listen, and answer the questions.**

1 What animals can the children see?
2 What's the difference between a tiger and a jaguar?
3 What do sloths eat?
4 Why does Phoebe tell Patrick not to touch the frog?

**3** **Choose a word. Describe it for your partner to guess.**    It's a big cat that …

**1** Read about the Amazon rain forest and match the numbers with the categories.

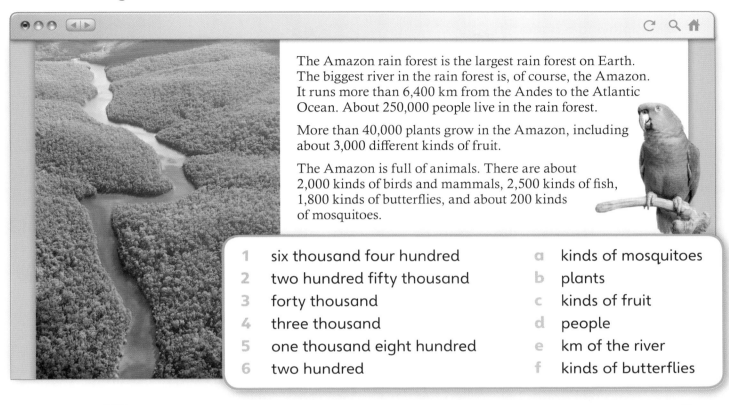

The Amazon rain forest is the largest rain forest on Earth. The biggest river in the rain forest is, of course, the Amazon. It runs more than 6,400 km from the Andes to the Atlantic Ocean. About 250,000 people live in the rain forest.

More than 40,000 plants grow in the Amazon, including about 3,000 different kinds of fruit.

The Amazon is full of animals. There are about 2,000 kinds of birds and mammals, 2,500 kinds of fish, 1,800 kinds of butterflies, and about 200 kinds of mosquitoes.

| | | | |
|---|---|---|---|
| 1 | six thousand four hundred | a | kinds of mosquitoes |
| 2 | two hundred fifty thousand | b | plants |
| 3 | forty thousand | c | kinds of fruit |
| 4 | three thousand | d | people |
| 5 | one thousand eight hundred | e | km of the river |
| 6 | two hundred | f | kinds of butterflies |

**2** CD 1 29  **Language focus** **Listen and say the numbers.**

100 – one hundred
1,000 – one thousand
10,000 – ten thousand
100,000 – one hundred thousand
1,000,000 – one million

500 – five hundred
3,000 – three thousand
40,000 – forty thousand
200,000 – two hundred thousand
5,000,000 – five million

**3** Work with a partner. Write and say.

Two hundred thousand.

**1** **Look at the pictures and answer the question.**

Mia is playing a game. She is a monkey lost in the jungle. What do you think she has to do?

**2**  **Read and listen to the dialog to check your answer.**

**Charlie** What are you playing?

**Mia** Oh, hi, Charlie! It's a new computer game I just got. It's called *Jungle Jake*. It's pretty cool.

**Charlie** What do you have to do?

**Mia** Well, you're a baby monkey called Jake. You're lost in the jungle, and you're trying to find your mom.

**Charlie** Is that all?

**Mia** Of course not. You have to do loads of other things.

**Charlie** Like what?

**Mia** Well, you have to find other animals, like sloths and toucans, and ask them for help.

**Charlie** OK, I get it.

**Mia** And you have to be careful of jaguars.

**Charlie** Why is that?

**Mia** Because they eat you, silly!

**Charlie** Is there anything else?

**Mia** Um, yes, you have to find bananas to eat. They give you energy. Do you want to give it a try?

**Charlie** No, I'm OK, thanks.

**Mia** Don't you like computer games?

**Charlie** I like games – I just don't like bananas.

**3** **Work in pairs.**

a Practice the dialog.

b Choose one of the computer games below and think of some rules for it. Make notes.

    *Anaconda!*    *Anthony the Anteater*    *Toucan Trees*

c Use your new game to make up your own dialog.

d Act out your dialog for the class.

 **What to say**

**Asking for instructions**
What do you have to do?
Is that all?
Is there anything else?

## 1 CD1 34 Listen and read the dialog. Then check (✓) the correct pictures.

| | |
|---|---|
| **Guide** | OK, Mr. Nelson, the tour starts at seven. So you have to be here at half past six. OK? |
| **Mr. Nelson** | Fine! What should I wear, a T-shirt? |
| **Guide** | No, no. There are lots of mosquitoes, so you have to wear a shirt with long sleeves. |
| **Mr. Nelson** | Oh, that's right. I had to wear a shirt when I went on a jungle tour a few years ago. Are my sneakers all right? |
| **Guide** | No, sorry. There are dangerous snakes around, so you have to wear boots. |
| **Mr. Nelson** | Do I have to bring food and something to drink? |
| **Guide** | You don't have to bring any food or water. We provide everything you need. |
| **Mr. Nelson** | That's great. Thanks. |

## 2 CD1 35 Grammar focus — Listen and say the sentences.

You **have to** wear a shirt with long sleeves.
I **had to** wear a shirt and boots.
Do I **have to** bring any food?
You **don't have to** bring any food.

## 3 Write *yes* or *no*. Then talk about the rules at your home with your partner.

1 help in the kitchen _____
2 go shopping _____
3 take off your shoes in the house _____
4 make your bed _____
5 clean your room _____
6 do the dishes _____

Do you have to help in the kitchen?

Yes, I do.

Do you have to go shopping?

No, I don't, but I like going shopping with my dad.

**1** **Work in pairs. Look at the pictures and the title of the story.**

a Where are the children this time?

b Who are they going to meet in the story?

**2** CD 1 36 **Read and listen to the story to check your answers.**

# The present

The children started walking through the rain forest looking for a way out. After half an hour, they came to a river. "I'm very hungry," said Alex. "Me, too," Phoebe and Patrick answered. "Let's follow the river, maybe we can find a village," Alex said. The three friends walked along the river in the rain forest for an hour. They were hot and hungry.

Suddenly they heard a very loud animal noise. "That must be a jaguar," Patrick shouted. "Let's climb that big tree over there to hide." They ran to the tree and started climbing. To their surprise, the terrible noise got louder and louder until it was right above their heads. They looked up into the tree and saw hairy black arms and a tail above them. "It's a howler monkey," Phoebe shouted. They all started to laugh. "That was a scary ten minutes!"

The children climbed down the tree and continued walking for 20 minutes. Suddenly Patrick stopped. "Look," he whispered, "there's a man with a spear." "We have to put our hands on our chest. That means we are friends," Phoebe said. The man smiled, and the three friends followed him. After 15 minutes, they saw some huts and a small village. In the middle, there was a fire with some women and small children sitting around it.

Two men appeared, and they took the children to a very old man. "I think that the old man is the chief, so we have to give him a present," Phoebe said. Alex gave his penknife to the old man. The old man looked very happy, and he pointed at the fire. The children went over and had some delicious food.

After dinner, a man took Phoebe, Alex, and Patrick to a nearby waterfall. He pointed to the top of it, and there they could see a yellow glow!

"We have to get there fast, or we'll never get back home!" Phoebe said. They smiled to say thank you to the man and started climbing. The problem was that the yellow gate was far out in the air. There was only one way to get to it. "We have to swing through the gate on a creeper," Patrick said. "I can't do that," Alex answered. "I'm scared." "Follow me," shouted Patrick. He grabbed a creeper, ran, swung through the air, and disappeared through the yellow glow.

Phoebe looked at Alex. "Let's go together," Alex said. "Hurry!" The two friends took the creeper, ran, and jumped. They were gone in a flash.

**3** **Read and check (✓) the correct name.**

|  | Phoebe | Alex | Patrick |
|---|---|---|---|
| 1 Who thought there was a jaguar? |  |  |  |
| 2 Who saw the man with the spear? |  |  |  |
| 3 Who gave the chief a present? |  |  |  |
| 4 Who was scared of jumping through the gate? |  |  |  |
| 5 Who helped Alex jump through the gate? |  |  |  |

**4** **Think!** **Read the story again and answer the question.**

How much time passed from the beginning of their adventure (when they started their walk through the rain forest) until they arrived in the village?

**Skills**

**1**  CD 2 02    **Listen to the documentary and complete the trading cards.**

**Killer Creatures**

**Jungle series 2**

NAME: Goliath bird-eating spider

WHERE: Northern _____ _____

SIZE: _____ cm

EATS: _____ , _____ ,

_____ , _____

LIVES FOR: _____ (female only)

**WARNING!** This is a very aggressive spider. It's poisonous, too!

**Killer Creatures**

**Jungle series 2**

NAME: Bengal tiger

WHERE: _____

SIZE: _____ m

EATS: buffalo, _____ ,

_____ , _____

LIVES FOR: _____

**WARNING!** There aren't many tigers left in the wild. They need our help now!

**2**  CD 2 03    **Listen again and answer the questions.**

1   How long do male spiders live?

2   What does the female spider do to the male?

3   What are the four big cats?

4   How many Bengal tigers are left in the wild?

**3**   **Use the trading card to write a short text about the king cobra.**

> The king cobra is from India and Southeast Asia.

**Killer Creatures**

**Jungle series 2**

NAME: King cobra

WHERE: India and Southeast Asia

SIZE: 6.5 m

EATS: Rats and other snakes

LIVES FOR: 20 years

**WARNING!** Can kill a human with one bite!

**4**   **Discuss in pairs.**

a   Which of these creatures would you most like to see? Why?

b   Which would you not like to see? Why?

> I'd like to see ...

**1** **Read the article and answer the questions. Give reasons for your answers.**

1 Were the men from the tribe surprised to see the plane?

2 Were the men from the tribe happy to see the plane?

3 Were the scientists on the plane surprised to see the tribe?

4 Were the scientists on the plane happy to see the tribe?

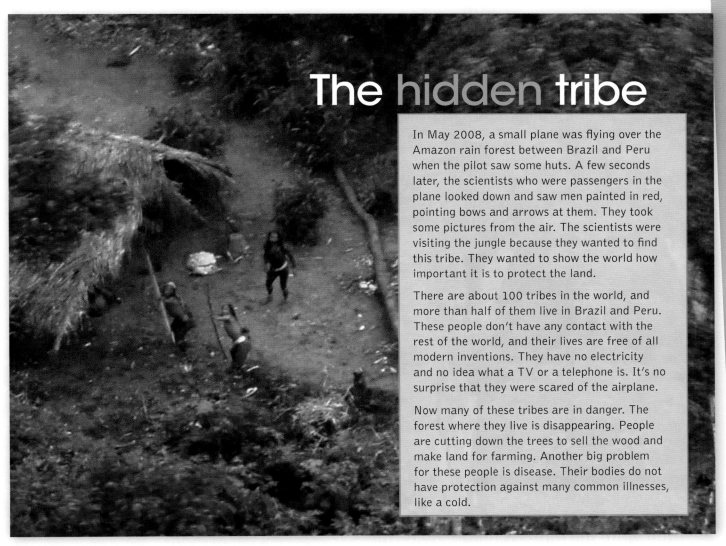

# The hidden tribe

In May 2008, a small plane was flying over the Amazon rain forest between Brazil and Peru when the pilot saw some huts. A few seconds later, the scientists who were passengers in the plane looked down and saw men painted in red, pointing bows and arrows at them. They took some pictures from the air. The scientists were visiting the jungle because they wanted to find this tribe. They wanted to show the world how important it is to protect the land.

There are about 100 tribes in the world, and more than half of them live in Brazil and Peru. These people don't have any contact with the rest of the world, and their lives are free of all modern inventions. They have no electricity and no idea what a TV or a telephone is. It's no surprise that they were scared of the airplane.

Now many of these tribes are in danger. The forest where they live is disappearing. People are cutting down the trees to sell the wood and make land for farming. Another big problem for these people is disease. Their bodies do not have protection against many common illnesses, like a cold.

**2** **Discuss with your partner. How do you think the chief of this tribe might answer these questions from a journalist?**

1 Why are you scared of us?

2 Do you want something from us?

3 Is your life better than ours?

**3** **In groups, present your ideas to the rest of the class.**

We're scared because …

# Help save the rain forest

**1** CD 2 05 **Think!** Why do you think rain forests are important? Write down as many answers as you can. Read and listen to the text and check your ideas.

* They are beautiful, so people like to go there on vacation.
* There are many rare plants and animals.

Rain forests are the lungs of our planet. They produce oxygen. Without oxygen, humans and animals would die.

Rain forests get their name because it rains a lot in them, and they store a lot of water. The trees take water from the forest floors and put it back into the air in the form of clouds. Without the rain forests, many parts of the world would not get any rain. Without rain, farmers could not produce food, and many people would die from hunger.

Rain forests are home to millions of plants and animals. If they get smaller, we'll lose many of these animals. The rain forests are also home to people who have lived in them for thousands of years. They, too, are in danger because the rain forests are getting smaller.

## Smart fact

Tropical rain forests are very old – between 60 million and 100 million years. Over 30 million different kinds of plants and animals live in them. That's half of Earth's wildlife and more than half of its different kinds of plants!

**2** Why are the rain forests in danger? Read and write the reasons under the pictures.

Thousands of trees are cut down in rain forests every day. This is called logging. Logging happens because people want to sell the trees. Wood from rain forest trees is expensive because it's very good quality.

Another problem is farming. Thousands of trees are cut down to create space for big farms. People around the world eat lots of meat. So more farms are needed, and that's bad for the rain forests.

Problem 1: _____

Problem 2: _____

(1) _____

(2) _____

(3) _____

(4) _____

(5) _____

(6) _____

(7) _____

**1** **Write the names of the continents on the map. Which of them have rain forests?**

Asia   North America   South America   Africa   Europe   Australia   Antarctica

**2** **Project** **Find out more about rain forests.**

1   Which continent do you live on? Is there a rain forest on your continent?

2   Use the Internet, talk to your teacher, or go to a library. What fascinating things can you see, hear, smell, taste, and touch in rain forests?

☐ ■ **A** *I* **A**                                                                        ● ● ●

In the rain forest you can:

see:          hear:          smell:          taste:          touch:

**3** **Now present your findings to the class.**

In the rain forest you can see trees and hear toucans …

## Act it out

# At the pet shop

**1 Work in pairs.
Choose a role card.**

**Student A**

**You are the customer.**
You want to buy an exotic pet – a snake, a spider, or a lizard. Think about the following:

- how much it costs
- if it's dangerous
- where to keep it and how much space the animal needs
- what to feed it and how often
- if you can play with it

**Student B**

**You are the owner of a pet shop.**
Someone is going to ask you questions about an exotic pet they want to buy. You tell the buyer:

- how much it is
- if it's dangerous or not
- where they should keep it and how big the tank should be
- how often they should feed it and what they should feed it
- if it is safe to play with the pet

**2 Act out your dialog.**

### Useful language

**Student A**

I'd like to buy …
How much … ?
Is it … ?
How big does the tank have to be … ?
What do I have to … ?
How often do I have to … ?
Is it safe to … ?

**Student B**

OK, what animal would you … ?
It's about … . It depends on the size.
Some are … others are …
The animal has to …
You have to …
They …

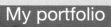

**My portfolio**

# A description

**1**  **Read Tim's message. Choose the best subject for the email.**

School!    My place    Friends and families    My hobbies

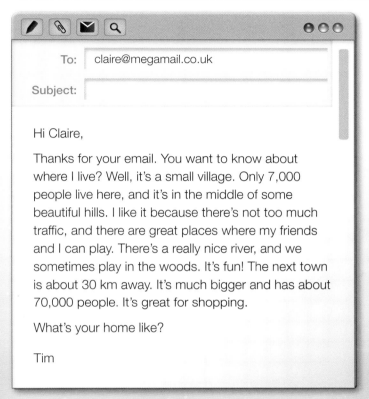

To: claire@megamail.co.uk

Subject:

Hi Claire,

Thanks for your email. You want to know about where I live? Well, it's a small village. Only 7,000 people live here, and it's in the middle of some beautiful hills. I like it because there's not too much traffic, and there are great places where my friends and I can play. There's a really nice river, and we sometimes play in the woods. It's fun! The next town is about 30 km away. It's much bigger and has about 70,000 people. It's great for shopping.

What's your home like?

Tim

**2**  **Find these words in Tim's email:** *fun, beautiful, small, great, nice.* **With a friend, read the email without these words. What does it sound like?**

**3**  **Choose five of the adjectives below to describe places in your town.**

quiet    long    huge    new
noisy    tiny    interesting
famous    unusual    old

**Tips for writers**

When you describe something, adjectives help you make your description better.

**4**  **Write an email to answer Tim. Use adjectives to describe your home.**

Hi Tim,

Thanks for your email. I'm going to tell you about where I live …

# 3 The rock 'n' roll show

In 1955, Elvis Presley was becoming a rock 'n' roll superstar. Many fans went to his shows. By 1956, he was the most popular singer in the U.S.A. and had his first number one hit record. He had more than 17 hits before he died in 1977. He still has a lot of fans today. For many people he will always be "The King."

1. spotlight
2. bodyguards
3. fans
4. electric guitar
5. bass guitar
6. backup singers
7. dancer
8. drum set
9. stage

**1** CD2 06 **Listen and say the words. Check with your partner.**

**2** CD2 07 **Read, listen, and complete the sentences.**

1. Patrick thinks they're in the _____ .
2. Patrick's _____ is a fan of Elvis Presley.
3. Alex prefers _____ _____ _____ .
4. _____ and _____ like the music.

places     people     objects

**3 Put the words from Activity 1 into three categories. Add two words of your own to each category.**

**1** CD 2 08  **Listen and read the interview. Write the months under the pictures.**

THE NEW QUEEN OF ROCK 'N' ROLL

(1) _____  (2) _____  (3) _____

**Interviewer** So Suzy, last year was a big year for you. What are your plans for this year?

**Suzy** Well, I'm making a new record right now, and it's going to be in the stores in April.

**Interviewer** That's great news.

**Suzy** And then in May, I'm going to go on a concert tour with my band.

**Interviewer** Which countries are you going to visit?

**Suzy** We're going to play in the U.K., France, Italy, Spain, and some other European countries.

**Interviewer** Are you going to play in the U.S.A.?

**Suzy** No, we're not going to play there this year. But we have plans to visit next year.

**Interviewer** So, a new record, a European tour. Is that everything for the year?

**Suzy** Well, I'm going to take a vacation in October. A nice long vacation …

**Interviewer** I hope you enjoy it.

**Suzy** Thanks!

**2** CD 2 09  **Grammar focus**  **Listen and say the sentences.**

I**'m going to** see the Suzy Slick show.
She's **not going to** play a concert in our town.
**Are you going to** buy the new Suzy Slick album?

**3** **Play the pop stars game. Ask and answer questions.**

- When / make / new album?
- What / call / it?
- When / play / show?
- Where / When / play / concerts?
- What / do / for the rest of the year?

What are you going to call your new album?

I'm going to call it *The King of the World*.

**1** CD2 10 **Listen and write the missing words. Then sing the song.**

I'm going to play a shiny (1) _____ ,
I'm going to drive a big fast car,
I'm going to go far, yeah, really far,
Because, baby, baby, baby ...
I'm going to be a (2) _____ .

Everyone's going to be my (3) _____ ,
Every woman and child and man,
I'm going to do everything I can,
Because, baby, baby, baby ...
I have a (4) _____ .

**All about music: Rock 'n' roll**

Rock 'n' roll started in the U.S.A. in the early 1950s. It was the first kind of music that was very popular with teenagers, and many older people did not like it. They thought music and dancing was bad for young people. Some of the most famous rock and rollers were Chuck Berry, Jerry Lee Lewis, and, of course, Elvis Presley.

**What I think**
▶ It's great.
⏸ It's OK.
✖ I don't really like it.

Rock, rock, come rock with me,
Yeah, roll, roll, roll with me,
Rock, rock, and you're going to see,
Just how big I'm going to be.

I'm going to shout. I'm going to (5) _____ ,
I'm going to do the dinga linga ling,
I'm going to win. Yeah, I'm going to win,
Because, baby, baby, baby ...
I'm going to be (6) _____ .

**2** CD2 12 **Listen and say the dialog.**

**Rose** Are you going to the rock 'n' roll show?
**Tom** I don't know, Rose. I prefer pop.
**Rose** But Tom! It's Joe and the Holey Socks!
**Tom** Well ... OK, why not?

**Joe and the Holey Socks**

Friday 6 p.m.

## 1 Read and match the pictures with the clocks.

# A day in the life of Suzy Slick
**Rock 'n' roll's newest superstar tells us how she spends her days.**

My alarm clock rings at twenty-five past nine, but I usually get up at half past. I'm so lazy! Then at ten o'clock I have a big breakfast of bacon and eggs, toast, and a fruit salad – the perfect start to the day. After breakfast, around twenty to eleven, I go to my computer and read my emails. I get lots from my fans, and I try to answer a few. Then I usually write my blog and go to the gym. At half past two, I make myself

a salad. Then I sit down at my piano and write songs. At a quarter past four I stop for half an hour and watch my favorite TV show. I never miss it.

At five o'clock I visit my hairdresser. In the evenings, sometimes I stay home and relax, and sometimes I go to parties with my friends. I never go to bed before midnight.

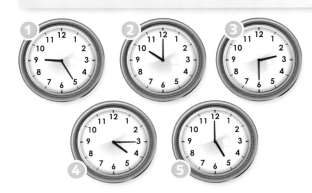

## 2 CD2 16 Language focus — Listen and say the times.

It's **five past** five.  It's **five to** six.  It's **ten past** five.  It's **ten to** six.

## 3 Play the time game.

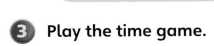

It's twenty to three.

Sorry. That's wrong. No points.

**1** **Go through the text quickly and find answers to the questions.**

a  Where do the children talk to Elvis?    b  Where do they have a meal with him?

**2** CD 2 17  **Read and listen to the story to check your answers.**

# ELVIS

After the show, the singer and his band left the stage. "Go on, Patrick," said Alex. "Ask him if he's Elvis." "Excuse me," asked Patrick. "Are you Elvis Presley, the king of rock 'n' roll?" The singer stopped. "Yes, I am," he said. He looked very happy. "I knew it!" said Patrick. "My grandma loves you." "Your grandma?" Elvis looked confused. "How old is your grandma?" "She's 70," Patrick said, "and she has all of your CDs." Now Elvis looked really confused. "What's a CD?" he asked. "Never mind," said Patrick. "I just wanted to tell you how much people love you."

Elvis invited the kids to his dressing room. They asked him about being famous. He said that it wasn't always as fun as it looked. "For example," he said, "how am I going to leave the theater with all those fans waiting? They're going to try to follow me to my hotel." The children listened. Even in the dressing room they could hear the fans. They were all shouting for Elvis. Alex looked around the room. "I have an idea," he said. "I'm going to need that long coat, those glasses, and that wig. Now listen carefully. Here's the plan … "

Outside the back door there were hundreds of fans waiting. When they saw Elvis, they all screamed and ran toward him. Soon they were all around him, taking pictures and trying to talk to him.

Suddenly Elvis took off his wig, glasses, and coat. The fans were amazed! Elvis wasn't Elvis! He was Alex sitting on the shoulders of Patrick. "Sorry, fans!" Patrick shouted. "Elvis wanted some peace and quiet." The two boys got into a car and drove away. Nobody followed them. At the same time, Elvis was walking out of the front of the theater with Phoebe, but nobody saw them.

Back at the hotel, Elvis thanked the kids with a fantastic American meal of hot dogs, hamburgers, ice cream, and milkshakes. Elvis was really funny and told them stories about being a rock 'n' roll star. They were having such a good time that Phoebe was sad when she noticed a familiar yellow glow. She turned to the boys, who were laughing with Elvis. "Sorry!" she said, "But we have to go." The boys were unhappy because they didn't really want to leave. Elvis watched as the children walked slowly toward the light. They turned to wave goodbye, and then they were gone in a flash.

**3** **Correct the mistakes in the sentences.**

1  Alex was the first to ask Elvis a question.
2  Patrick's mother is a fan of Elvis.
3  Elvis took the kids to a café to talk.
4  Alex used a wig, a coat, and a pair of boots for his plan.
5  Patrick wore the wig and the glasses.
6  Phoebe and Elvis left from the back of the theater.
7  The kids ate pizza and spaghetti with Elvis.
8  The children were happy to leave Elvis.

**4** **Think!** **Here are some Elvis songs that were big hits. Can you complete them with the words in the box?**

dog  It's  Blue  me  Let's

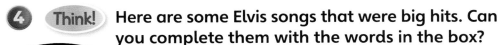

**1** CD 2 18  **Listen and choose the correct words.**

1   Buick / Chevy / Cadillac

3   Jukebox / Jivebox / Music box

2   Jive skirt / Swing skirt / Boogie skirt

**2** CD 2 19  **Listen again and answer the questions.**

1   When was the Cadillac Series 62 built?
2   How long was it?
3   What influenced the fashion of the fifties?
4   What did a lot of parents think of swing skirts?
5   How many records did a jukebox hold?
6   How did you work a jukebox?

**3**  **Talk about what you like best: the Cadillac, the swing skirt, or the jukebox. Why?**

> I like the jukebox because …

**Skills**

**1** **Look at the pictures and answer the questions.**

1 What is the girl with the guitar doing?

2 What do the boy and the other girls think of her?

**2** CD2 20 **Read, listen, and check your answers.**

**WANTED**
**ELECTRIC GUITARIST FOR THE**

**METAL KINGS**
**WE'RE GOING TO BE BIG!**
**CALL MIKE ON 970 2346.**

**Backup Singer wanted for**
**Girlz**
**We're going to the top!**
**Call Katia on 655 4348**

The poster was Misha's dream come true. She called and arranged to meet Mike. She was nervous as she walked into the room because the band looked like real rock stars. "I'm looking for Mike," said Misha. "I've come to join his band." "I'm Mike," said a man. "Let's hear you play." Misha started to play, but after 20 seconds, Mike asked her to stop. "You play well," he said, "but you're not loud enough. We're playing for Don Parsons next week. I don't think you'll help us get a contract with him." Misha left. She was sad.

Luckily, Misha saw another poster that could make her dream come true the next day. She arranged to meet Katia that afternoon. When she arrived, she was nervous. "I'm looking for Katia," Misha said, "I'd like to join her band." "Oh," said the girl, "I'm Katia. Sing me a song." After ten seconds, Katia didn't want to hear any more. "You sing well," she said, "but you don't look right. We're singing for Don Parsons next week. I don't think you'll help us get a contract with him."

Two weeks later, Misha was playing her guitar in the town center. She enjoyed playing for the shoppers. She looked up and noticed a well-dressed man watching her. When she finished, he came up and introduced himself. "I'm Don Parsons," he said, "I'm a record producer. I think you could be a star." Misha couldn't believe it. "But I'm too quiet to be a star." "No, you're not," Don said. "Lots of bands think that if they make a loud noise, they're good. I saw The Metal Kings last week – they were loud, but they weren't good." Misha still couldn't believe it. "But I don't look like a star." "You look perfect, and you can sing," Don said. "I saw Girlz last week – they looked good, but they couldn't sing." "But, but, but … ," said Misha. "But nothing! You have it all," said Don. "If you want to be a star, I can help you make it happen."

**3** **Match the sentence halves to make the summary.**

| | | | |
|---|---|---|---|
| 1 | First Misha sees an ad for | a | a guitarist. |
| 2 | They are looking for | b | a singer. |
| 3 | Mike thinks she | c | doesn't look right. |
| 4 | Next Misha sees an ad for | d | while she is playing the guitar. |
| 5 | They are looking for | e | is too quiet. |
| 6 | The girls think she | f | is perfect! |
| 7 | Misha meets Don Parsons | g | The Metal Kings. |
| 8 | Don Parsons thinks Misha | h | a band called Girlz. |

Value: not giving up; reading **41**

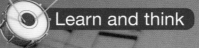

# Rhythm

CD 2 21

**1** Listen, read, and find out what you need to make rhythm. Number the sounds.

## What is rhythm?

Rhythm is all around us. You hear it when a basketball player bounces a ball, when the rain falls against the window, or when you clap your hands. Rhythm is very important in making music. It is made from sounds and silences. These sounds can be longer, louder, shorter, or quieter.

Some silences can be longer or shorter. When the sounds and silences are repeated, we get a pattern of sound that is called rhythm. In one piece of music, we can often hear more than one rhythm. Listen to the sounds. Can you hear the rhythm?

**2** CD 2 22 **Think!** Listen to three short rhythms and write numbers 1–3. Then listen and clap.

|     |     |     |     |     |
| --- | --- | --- | --- | --- |
| ___ | xx  | xx  | xx  | xx  |
| ___ | X   | xx  | X   | xx  |
| ___ | X   | X   | X   | X   |

snake – monkey – snake – monkey

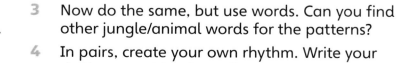

**3** The girl in the picture is saying a rhythm. Which of the rhythms in Activity 2 is she saying?

**4** Make each of the three rhythms using the two words *snake* (X) and *monkey* (xx).

1 Work in three groups. Each group claps one of the rhythms in Activity 2.

2 Now the three groups clap their different rhythms at the same time.

3 Now do the same, but use words. Can you find other jungle/animal words for the patterns?

4 In pairs, create your own rhythm. Write your rhythm on a big piece of paper.

5 Clap it to the class.

**1** Read the text. Write the correct words under the music notes and complete the sentence.

### Rhythm in music

To show rhythm in music we use quarter notes ( ♩ ) and eighth notes ( ♪ ).

♩   ♫   ♩   ♫

A quarter note is one beat. An eighth note is half a beat. So two eighth notes are the same length as one quarter note.

♩                      ♫

one _____    two _____

A quarter note is the length of _____

**2** CD2 24 Try clapping each of these rhythms. Then listen and check.

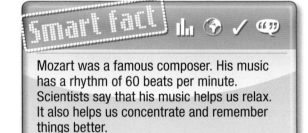

**Smart fact**

Mozart was a famous composer. His music has a rhythm of 60 beats per minute. Scientists say that his music helps us relax. It also helps us concentrate and remember things better.

**3** Use the words *snake* and *monkey* to say each of the rhythms in Activity 2.

**4** Project Music and my learning.

**DAY 1**

1 Choose a piece of text (about 80 words) that you want to remember from this book.

2 Listen to some music by Mozart. Study the text for ten minutes.

3 Half an hour later ask someone to test you. How much did you remember? Give yourself points.

  1 nothing at all
  2 a little
  3 a lot
  4 everything

**DAY 2**

1 Choose another piece of text (80 words) from this book. Study it for ten minutes, but this time don't play any music.

2 Half an hour later ask someone to test you. Give yourself points and write them down.

3 Add up your points. Talk about your findings in class.

**Time to present**

# A show-and-tell

**1**  **CD 2 26** Listen to Jasmine talking about her favorite singer and make notes.

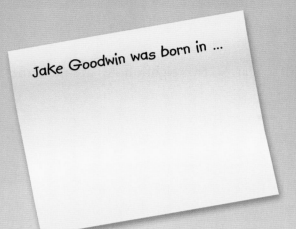

Jake Goodwin was born in ...

**2** **What does Jasmine like about Jake Goodwin besides his music?**

Jasmine likes ...

## Find out about it

- Talk to your friends. Find out who their favorite singers or bands are.
- Listen to some of the songs they like.
- Choose a singer or band for your presentation.

## Prepare it

- Find out more about the singer/group: name, country, language(s), hobbies, most successful song, how many songs, family ... .
- Think about these questions and write down your answers:
  - Where do you listen to music – on the Internet, CDs, friends' CDs, the radio?
  - Which songs do you like best? What do you like about them?
  - Collect some pictures from magazines or the Internet.

## Present it

- You should talk for about a minute. Show the pictures. Think about questions you can ask your classmates.

Do you like ... ?

Did you know that ... ?

 **Tips for presenters**

If you want to use a difficult word in your talk, write it on the board before you start. Use the word in a sentence. Can your friends guess what it means?

# A diary

**1** **Read Jeremy's diary and put the paragraphs in the correct order.**

☐ Then we rode to Whitewall Castle. There is a huge park with a little lake in the middle. We had a picnic.

☐ So we went home fast. We were wet, but it was a wonderful day.

☐ Last Sunday, a group of friends and I went on a bike ride.

☐ Finally, we went to the stadium to see a soccer game. But the weather changed, and it started to rain.

☐ First, we rode up into the hills close to our town. It was great up there. The weather was beautiful.

**2** **Add these words to make Kylie's diary better.**

first    finally    last Sunday    then

## SATURDAY

Grandma and Grandpa came to visit me and my sister. We went to the fun park in Blackhill. Grandma went on the haunted house with us. That was fantastic. We walked to a very nice restaurant and had lunch there. I had chicken and French fries, and my sister had a burger. We went to the town hall. There was a concert with Give It All. They are a new band from Liverpool. The concert was great. We were very tired and went home right away. We went to bed at eight o'clock.

> **Tips for writers**
>
> When you want to say that something happened in the past (last weekend, last summer, in 2011, three weeks ago … ), use verbs in their past forms: *was/were … had … went … didn't like … stayed … loved.*

**3** **Think about something you did last weekend.**

**a** Write about it for five minutes. Just write, write, write. When you can't think of a word, make a line _____ . You can add the word later.

**b** Think how you can organize your ideas. Use the words from Activity 2 to do this.

**c** Put your text in an envelope and seal it. Look at it again after three days and try to make it even better.

# 4 Space restaurant

What will people eat in the year 3002? Nobody knows. Maybe they will eat pills when they are hungry. Red pills in the morning, blue pills at lunchtime, and green pills in the evening. Maybe people on Earth will get all their food out of machines.

1. waiter
2. cookies
3. salt
4. pepper
5. napkin
6. chopsticks
7. fork
8. spoon
9. knife

**1** CD2 27 Listen and say the words. Check with your partner.

**2** CD2 28 **Read, listen, and answer the questions.**

1 When do they serve meals in the restaurant?
2 How is time different?
3 What is the date?
4 How old is Phoebe?

**3** **Choose words and play the odd-one-out game with your partner.**

My words are knife, salt, and chopsticks.

Salt is the odd one out. You don't use it to eat.

# 1 Read the email and answer the questions.

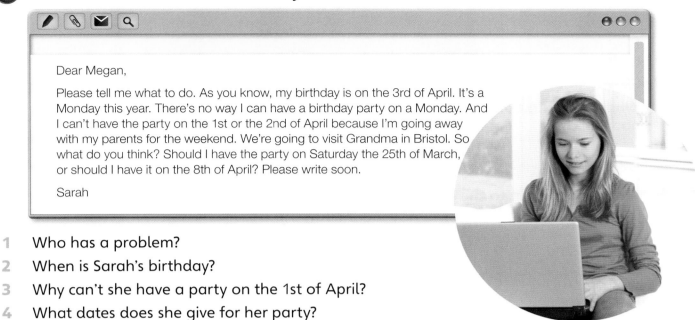

Dear Megan,

Please tell me what to do. As you know, my birthday is on the 3rd of April. It's a Monday this year. There's no way I can have a birthday party on a Monday. And I can't have the party on the 1st or the 2nd of April because I'm going away with my parents for the weekend. We're going to visit Grandma in Bristol. So what do you think? Should I have the party on Saturday the 25th of March, or should I have it on the 8th of April? Please write soon.

Sarah

1   Who has a problem?
2   When is Sarah's birthday?
3   Why can't she have a party on the 1st of April?
4   What dates does she give for her party?

# 2 CD2 29   Language focus   Listen and say the sentences.

This year the **1st (first)** of May is a Monday.
The **2nd (second)** of May is a Tuesday.
The **3rd (third)** of May is a Wednesday.
The **4th (fourth)** of May is a Thursday.
The **5th (fifth)** of May is a Friday.

# 3 Think!   Work with a partner. Ask and answer.

JUNE
**30**
MONDAY

July

|    |    |    |    |    |    |
|----|----|----|----|----|----|
| 1  | 2  | 3  | 4  | 5  | 6  |
| 7  | 8  | 9  | 10 | 11 | 12 | 13 |
| 14 | 15 | 16 | 17 | 18 | 19 | 20 |
| 21 | 22 | 23 | 24 | 25 | 26 | 27 |
| 28 | 29 | 30 | 31 |    |    |    |

What day is the 11th of July?

Give me a second. I think it's a Friday.

That's right.

# 4 Think of three questions to ask your partner.

When is your dad's birthday?

What is the last day of school this year?

**1** Look at the pictures and answer the questions.

- How does Charlie look in picture 1 and picture 2?

- What do you think happened?

**2**  Read and listen to the dialog to check your answers. Complete with the missing numbers from the box.

> 5th   22nd   29th

| | |
|---|---|
| **Charlie** Hey, Josh, isn't it your birthday soon? | **Charlie** I love that place. |
| **Josh** Um, yes. It's on the (1)_____ . | **Josh** Yeah, it is pretty good. |
| **Charlie** What! That's only a week away. Today's the (2)_____ . | **Charlie** So what do you want for a birthday present? Are you still into Mega Monster trading cards? |
| **Josh** Yeah, I know. | **Josh** Yeah, I still like them. |
| **Charlie** So what are you going to do? Are you going to have a party? | **Charlie** Excellent! I'll get you three packets. |
| **Josh** Not this year. Mom said I could take some friends to the movies. | **Josh** Um, Charlie, there's one problem. |
| **Charlie** Cool! What movie? | **Charlie** What's that? |
| **Josh** *KidSpyz 3.* | **Josh** Mom said I can only have four friends, and you were (3)_____ on the list. I'm sorry. |
| **Charlie** Great! I really want to see that one. | **Charlie** Oh, no! |
| **Josh** And then we're going to have lunch at Benny's. | **Josh** I'm only joking, Charlie. You were first on my list! |

**3** Work in pairs.

a Practice the dialog.

b Imagine one of you has a birthday soon. Decide on:
- when it is
- a good way to celebrate
- what would be a good present
- how many people are invited

c Use your ideas to make up your own dialog.

d Act out your dialog for the class.

**?** **What to say**

**Expressing excitement**
What!
So what are you going to do?
Cool!
Great!
I love that …
Excellent!

**1** **Read and correct the sentences below.**

## Food will never be the same again.

By our reporter Poppy Beanie

Yesterday, in his laboratory, Professor McKarrot showed us what our food will be like in the future.

"Look at these two pills. If you put water on the green pill, you get broccoli with fish," the professor said. The professor poured water on the green pill. But there was a problem. The fish was green, too. The professor was not happy.

"If you put water on the pink pill, you get tomatoes with beef," the professor said. Then he poured water on the pink pill. The tomatoes looked like pink roses, and the beef looked like pink paper. "We're working on it," the professor told us, "we're not quite there."

1 Poppy Beanie is a scientist.
2 Professor McKarrot showed her how to make food in the future.
3 If you put coffee on the green pill, you get broccoli with fish.
4 If you put water on the pink pill, you get tomatoes with chicken.

**2**  Grammar focus **Listen and say the sentences.**

> If you **put** honey in your tea, it **becomes** sweet.
> If you **leave** chocolate in the sun, it **becomes** very soft.
> If you **put** water in the freezer, it **turns** to ice.

**3** **Play the food game with a partner. Imagine that you have pills of six different colors. Tell your partner what food you get.**

If you put water on the blue pill, you get potatoes with spinach.

**1** Look at the pictures. Where can you see these things?

1 knives and forks  2 lots of dishes to do  3 a birthday cake  4 pots with steam

**2**  Go through the text quickly. Why does the robot want the children to do the dishes? Listen and check your answer.

# The birthday meal

The friends sat down at the table. After ten minutes, the waiter came with the starter. There were three bowls with something orange in them. "Orange soup with fish and pepper," the waiter said. They tried to eat the soup with their spoons, but it didn't work. The soup was hard. "If you throw your soup into the air, you can eat it more easily," said the waiter. So they threw the soup out of the bowls into the air. The soup fell onto the table and broke into hundreds of little orange balls. The children tried to pick up the balls with their spoons, but they always rolled away. "It's easier if you use your chopsticks," the waiter said. So they ate the little balls with their chopsticks.

"The soup is really good," Phoebe said. "It tastes like fishy, peppery candies." "I like it, too," Alex agreed, "but I'm still hungry."

The waiter came in with the second course. There were four big pots with lids on. When the waiter took the lids off, colored steam came out of them. "Beef, carrots, broccoli, and crocodile," he said. "You have to eat the steam fast, or it will disappear." The children took their spoons and tried to eat the steam as fast as possible, but they didn't get much.

"I can't believe that all we have to eat is soup and steam!" said Alex. "What's for dessert?" the children asked. "Wait and see," answered the waiter.

The kitchen door opened with a loud noise. Phoebe, Alex, and Patrick saw a huge spaceship sailing toward them. On it there were lots and lots of burning candles. "Happy birthday!" shouted the waiter as the spaceship landed in front of Phoebe.

"Blow out the candles," Alex said. "Please help me," answered Phoebe, "there are too many." So together they blew out the candles. "Hooray! The spaceship is made of chocolate, and there's ice cream inside," Phoebe shouted. Alex, Patrick, and Phoebe ate until they were full.

"That was wonderful," Phoebe said. Right then the waiter came and gave them the bill. "It's 60,000 goldstars altogether," he said.

"What? We, we … don't have any goldstars," Patrick answered. The waiter scratched his head. "Then I'm afraid that you have to work in the kitchen for a week." The children nodded sadly and walked toward the kitchen. When they got to the door, a golden glow appeared around it. They looked at each other happily and walked into it. They were gone in a flash.

**3** **Read and answer the questions.**

1 What was the first course?

2 How could they catch the orange balls?

3 What was the second course?

4 What did they have for dessert?

5 What money does the restaurant take?

6 What did the waiter tell them to do?

**4** **Think!** **Read and match the prices with the objects.**

If a three-course meal for three costs 60,000 goldstars, how much do you think these things cost at the edge of the universe?

1,000 goldstars   10,000 goldstars   50,000 goldstars   100,000 goldstars

1
A can of space cola

2
A trip to the 6D movies

3
A jet booster bike

4
A pet zonk

**1** Read the blog and match the pictures with the paragraphs.

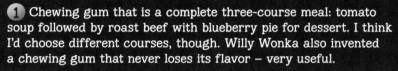

# TheChocolateBlog.com
## for all things sweet and chocolatey

I'm crazy about chocolate, so it's no surprise that my favorite book is *Charlie and the Chocolate Factory* by the wonderful Roald Dahl. Forget Charlie Bucket, the real hero of the book is Willy Wonka, inventor of the most amazing candies in the world. Here are just a few of his delicious creations:

**1** Chewing gum that is a complete three-course meal: tomato soup followed by roast beef with blueberry pie for dessert. I think I'd choose different courses, though. Willy Wonka also invented a chewing gum that never loses its flavor – very useful.

**2** Hot ice cream for a cold day! What a great idea. Now I can eat ice cream every day! He also invented ice cream that never melts – very useful.

**3** Wallpaper that you can lick. This wallpaper comes with pictures of fruit all over it; oranges, grapes, apples, bananas. When you lick the pictures, you taste the fruit. Fantastic!

**4** Lollipops with lights in them – perfect for eating in bed and reading at night.

**5** Grass made of sugar, called Swudge. It grows by the chocolate river and the chocolate waterfall in Willy Wonka's factory.

**6** Mr. Wonka also invented some great candies for schoolchildren, such as invisible chocolate bars. The teacher doesn't know you are eating them! There are also sugar-coated pencils and magic hand-fudge – you hold the fudge in your hand, and you taste it in your mouth. Finally, there are Wonka's exploding candies – a great way to scare the school bully!

Anyway, these are just a few of his inventions. Read the book if you want to know more.

**2** Discuss in small groups.

a Which of the candies would you like most? Why? I'd like to try ...

b What three courses would you like your chewing gum to be?

c What flavors would you like on your wallpaper?

## How to make

# A hot chocolate Swudge drink
straight from Willy Wonka's factory!

**1** **Write the words under the pictures.**

| an ice cream glass | an ice cream scoop | a pan | a straw |

You need:

_____  _____  _____  _____

**2** CD 2 36 **Listen and write the missing numbers.**

❶

___ bottle(s) of chocolate sauce

❷

___ bag(s) of green jelly candies

❸

___ g of milk chocolate

❹

___ ml of cream

❺

___ tablespoon(s) of sugar

❻

___ ball(s) of chocolate-mint ice cream

**3** CD 2 37 **Listen and put the steps in order.**

☐ Fill a quarter of the glass with chocolate sauce.

☐ Pour some more chocolate sauce on top of the ice cream so that it runs down the ice cream like a chocolate waterfall.

☐ Cut the jelly candies to make blades of grass.

☐ Put in a straw and start drinking!

☐ Break the chocolate and slowly melt it in a pan. Add the cream and the sugar and mix them together. Don't let it get too hot and keep stirring!

☐ When the chocolate, cream, and sugar, are well mixed, pour the mixture into the glass containing the chocolate sauce. Now add the ice cream.

**4** **Work in pairs. Think of something you would like to invent.**

● What is it called?

● What are the ingredients?

● How do you make it?

**5** **Present your invention to the class.**

# The importance of eating healthy food

**1** **Look at the pictures. Which child is healthier? Why do you think this?**

**2** **Read the text. Think of a short title for it.**

_____

Food keeps you alive. If you don't eat, your body won't work, but that's not enough. You want your body to be in good shape and to work well. It can only work well if you choose healthy food.

**Healthy food helps:**

- make your bones and muscles strong.
- repair damage.
- give you the energy you need.
- keep your digestion healthy (how the food gets through your body).
- keep you warm.

**3**  **Read and listen to the text. Look at the picture and think about what you eat.**

**Look at the picture of different food groups that we eat. The plate shows the correct amounts you need of each food group.**

- Fruits and vegetables make you strong and give you energy.
- Grains are good for your digestion.
- Dairy products are good for your bones and teeth.
- Proteins give you energy and help repair your body.
- Sugars taste great, but are not very good for you!

Fruits and vegetables

Grains

Proteins

Sugars

Dairy products

**1** **Think!** **Read these food words. Name the food groups.**

Group a is ...

a | mango    pineapple    strawberry | _____

b | onions    carrots    tomatoes | _____

c | turkey    pork    eggs | _____

d | wheat    corn    rice | _____

e | butter    cream    yogurt | _____

**2** **Match some of the words with the pictures.**

1 _____  2 _____  3 _____  4 _____  5 _____

**3** **Think!** **Write two other foods that you could add to each category.**

**4** **Project** **Think!** **What I eat in a week.**

1 Make a chart for each day of the week. List all the things you eat on that day.

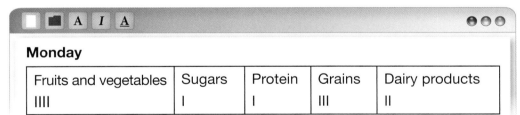

**Monday**

| Fruits and vegetables IIII | Sugars I | Protein I | Grains III | Dairy products II |
|---|---|---|---|---|

2 At the end of the week, count your points for each category.

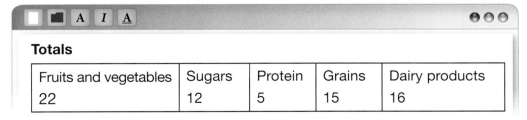

**Totals**

| Fruits and vegetables 22 | Sugars 12 | Protein 5 | Grains 15 | Dairy products 16 |
|---|---|---|---|---|

3 Think about what you ate. Could you eat more or less of some categories?

# Act it out

## At the restaurant

**1** **Work in pairs.**
**Choose a role card.**

**Student A**

**You are the customer.**
You are having a meal in a restaurant. Think about the following:

- saying hello
- asking for the menu
- ordering something to drink
- ordering starters
- ordering the main course
- ordering another drink
- ordering dessert
- asking for the bill
- saying goodbye

**Student B**

**You are the waiter/waitress.**
Think about the following:

- saying hello to the guests and showing them a table
- bringing the menu
- asking what they would like to drink
- asking what they would like to eat
- asking if they would like anything else
- asking if everything was all right
- bringing the bill
- saying thank you

**2** **Act out your dialog.**

## Useful language

**Student A**

Hello, do you have a table for … ?
I'd like to see …
What do you suggest?
For starters I'd like …
Then I'll have …
Can I have … with the … ?
Can I have another … ?
Could you please bring me … ?
Can I have … ?

**Student B**

Please follow me.
What would you like … ?
Can I suggest the … ?
The … is very good.
You certainly can.
Of course.
Is everything … ?
Here's the …

# A recipe

**1** **Read the recipe.**

**a** Complete the text with the phrases from the box.

**b** Match the words (1–4) with the pictures.

Things you need   Ingredients   How to make it

## Apple Surprise

**Preparation time:** 10 minutes

**(1)** _____

2 small red apples
2 tbsp.* lemon juice
2 tbsp. sugar
a pinch of cinnamon
some vanilla ice cream

**(2)** _____

**1** knife    **2** a tablespoon
**3** blender    **4** serving bowls

**(3)** _____

● Peel the apples and cut them into small pieces. Throw away the core.

● Put the apple pieces and lemon juice into the blender. Blend until the mixture is very smooth.

● Pour the mixture into a small bowl and stir in the sugar and cinnamon.

● Pour over your ice cream and enjoy!

### Note:
Use a knife only when a parent or another adult is present!

*tbsp. = tablespoon

**2** **Circle the verbs in "How to make it" and write them under the pictures.**

**1**    **2**

**3**    **4**

**5**

**3** **Write your own recipe. Include information about _Ingredients_, _Preparation time_, _Things you need_, and _How to make it_. Find a good name for your recipe.**

 **Tips for writers**

When you create your own recipe, use verbs such as: _put in, stir, peel, cut, pour._

Use the following language to say how much: _a pinch of, a tablespoon of, a cup of, half a liter of, half a kilo of._

# 5 The Wild West

The Wild West describes part of North America in the second half of the 19th century. It was a time when people were traveling across North America, discovering new land, and building new towns. It was also the time of cowboys, both good and bad!

1. jail
2. sheriff
3. robbers
4. wagon
5. handcuffs
6. barrel
7. pistol
8. saddle
9. rope

**1** CD 2 39 **Listen and say the words. Check with your partner.**

**2** CD 2 40 **Read, listen, and complete the sentences.**

1 Patrick loves _____ .
2 Alex thinks the men on horses are _____ .
3 The sheriff is wearing a _____ and has a _____ in his holster.
4 Phoebe thinks the sheriff looks _____ .

**3** **Choose a word. Describe it for your partner to guess.**

You find this on a horse.

Is it a … ?

## 1 Match the sentences with the pictures.

1 It's made of wood and metal.
2 It's made of cotton.
3 They're made of leather.
4 It's used for hiding your face.
5 They're made of glass.
6 They're used for keeping your feet warm.
7 They're used for holding water.
8 It's used for traveling to places.

## 2 CD 3 02 Grammar focus — Listen and say the sentences.

The saddle's **made of** leather. It's **used for** riding horses.
The handcuffs **are made of** metal. They're **used for** arresting robbers.

## 3 Play the guessing game.

I'm thinking of an object.  Is it made of wood?

**1** CD 3 03 **Listen and write the missing words. Then sing the song.**

His (1) _____ was made of silver,
His teeth were black and (2) _____ .
His name was Billie Liar,
The meanest robber in town.

When Billie rode along the (3) _____ ,
The people all got down,
And hid behind the (4) _____ ,
From the meanest robber in town.

Billie robbed a lot of (5) _____ ,
He went from town to town.
Not a single (6) _____ was ever safe,
From the meanest robber in town.

One day he robbed a (7) _____ ,
As it came into the town,
And that was the one (8) _____ ,
From the meanest robber in town.

Sitting inside the stagecoach,
Dressed in (9) _____ and brown,
Was (10) _____ William Teller,
The quickest man in town.

The sheriff grabbed the robber,
And threw him to the ground.
Now Billy Liar's behind the (11) _____
Of the safest jail in town.

**All about music: Country and Western**

Country and western music came from the U.S.A. in the 1920s. The songs were often about cowboys and told stories of the early settlers. These days the music is still very popular in America and in many other parts of the world as well.

**What I think**
- ▶ It's great.
- ❚❚ It's OK.
- ✗ I don't really like it.

**2** CD 3 06 **Listen and say the dialog.**

**Eddie**  Run, Jenny! Billie's getting out his gun!
**Jenny**  Well, I'm not running, Eddie. He has a bubble gun!

**1** Follow the lines and write *t* (true) or *f* (false).

1 The sheriff's badge is made of silver.
2 The sheriffs' badges are made of gold.
3 The baby's horse is brown.
4 The babies' horses are gray.
5 The child's scarf is blue.
6 The children's scarves are red.

**2**  **Grammar focus** **Listen and say the sentences.**

| | |
|---|---|
| The **sheriff's** badge. | The **sheriffs'** badges. |
| The **baby's** hat. | The **babies'** hats. |
| The **child's** T-shirt. | The **children's** T-shirts. |
| The **man's** book. | The **men's** books. |

**3** Look at the picture on page 58 and write sentences. How many sentences can you write in three minutes?

- the robbers
- the sheriff
- the children
- the babies

*The robbers' horses are ...*

Possessive apostrophes **61**

**1** Go through the text quickly and find answers to the questions.

   **a**   What are the names of the robbers?      **b**   What does the sheriff give the kids?

**2** *CD 3 / 10*    Read and listen to the story to check your answers.

# The bank robbery

The children watched the men get off their horses and walk up to the bank. The people in the street looked very worried and went inside their houses. The men had scarves around their mouths. They disappeared inside the bank.

"I don't like this," said Phoebe. "I think they're going to rob the bank." A minute later, a woman ran out of the building. "They're robbing the bank!" she shouted. "You were right, Phoebe," said Alex, "but what can we do?" "We can go in and stop them," said Patrick. "Don't be silly," said Phoebe. "That's too dangerous. Let's go and talk to the sheriff."

The kids went into the sheriff's office and told him about the robbers. He wasn't very interested. "Aren't you going to do something?" asked Phoebe. "What can I do?" asked the sheriff. "They're the Dalton brothers, the most dangerous robbers around. I'm not going to try to stop them. It's too dangerous!" "Well, somebody has to do something," said Patrick. "Come on, I have a plan!"

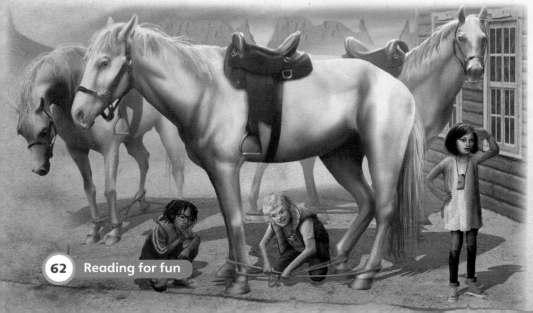

Patrick walked over to the robbers' horses. Phoebe and Alex followed. "Pass me that rope," he said. Alex gave him the rope, and Patrick tied it around the horses' legs. "That'll stop them!" he said. "I think we need to do more," said Alex. "Give me your penknife, Patrick." "Hurry up, boys," said Phoebe. "The Daltons are coming."

The Dalton brothers walked up to the children. "You three are brave," the tallest one said. He took out a big knife. The kids were scared. "Don't worry," he said. "This is to free our horses. Nice try, kids!" He cut the rope from the horses' legs, and they rode away. "That wasn't a very good plan!" Phoebe said. "Just wait a minute," said Alex.

As the Daltons were leaving town, their horses jumped over a fence, and the men fell to the ground. "We got them!" Alex shouted. "Get the sheriff."

The sheriff walked up to the brothers and put handcuffs on them. "That was very smart, kids, but how did you do it?" "I knew they had to jump over that fence to leave town," said Alex, "so I cut the straps on their saddles." The sheriff took the brothers to the jail and put them behind bars. He gave each of the kids a badge. "Thank you!" he said. As the kids walked past the jail door, the shortest of the brothers shouted out to them. "We'll get you kids!"

"I don't think so!" said Phoebe. She could see the yellow light glowing. "Goodbye, Dalton brothers. Goodbye, sheriff!" The Time Travelers walked into the light and were gone in a flash.

## 3 Choose the correct answers.

1 Who wants to go into the bank?

   a Alex   b Patrick   c Phoebe

2 Why doesn't the sheriff want to do anything?

   a He's scared.   b He's lazy.   c He's tired.

3 What does the tallest Dalton brother think of the kids?

   a They are silly.
   b They are courageous.
   c They are scared.

4 What does Alex do with the penknife?

   a He cuts the rope.
   b He stops the sheriff.
   c He cuts the saddles.

## 4 Think! Who do you think says these things? Where and when do they say them?

1 Everybody on the floor. Now give us the money.

2 The Dalton brothers aren't scared of me!

3 That was a great plan, Alex.

4 Those kids. They tricked us!

5 These brothers aren't going to rob any more banks now.

## Skills

**1** **Read the webpage and match the words with the definitions.**

1 teepee
2 Sioux
3 bison
4 reservations

a areas of land where modern Indians live
b an animal that lives in North America
c a famous Indian tribe
d a typical Indian house

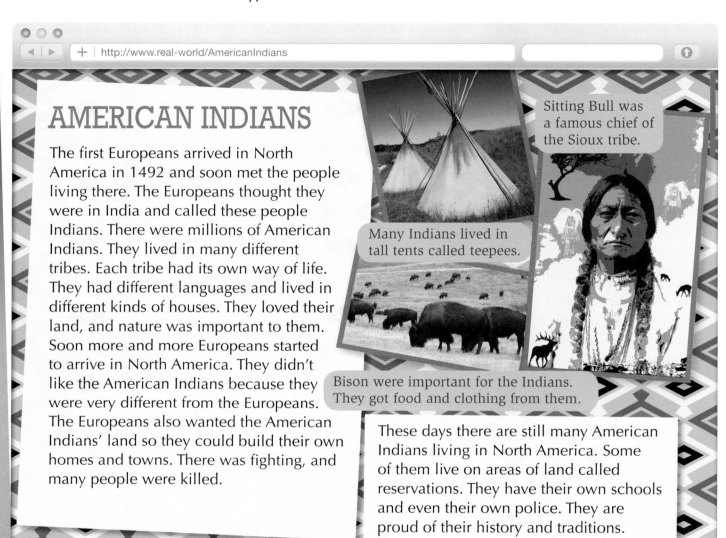

http://www.real-world/AmericanIndians

# AMERICAN INDIANS

The first Europeans arrived in North America in 1492 and soon met the people living there. The Europeans thought they were in India and called these people Indians. There were millions of American Indians. They lived in many different tribes. Each tribe had its own way of life. They had different languages and lived in different kinds of houses. They loved their land, and nature was important to them. Soon more and more Europeans started to arrive in North America. They didn't like the American Indians because they were very different from the Europeans. The Europeans also wanted the American Indians' land so they could build their own homes and towns. There was fighting, and many people were killed.

Sitting Bull was a famous chief of the Sioux tribe.

Many Indians lived in tall tents called teepees.

Bison were important for the Indians. They got food and clothing from them.

These days there are still many American Indians living in North America. Some of them live on areas of land called reservations. They have their own schools and even their own police. They are proud of their history and traditions.

**2** **Read the webpage again and discuss the questions.**

1 How did the American Indians get their name?
2 How were American Indian tribes different from each other?
3 Why did things get bad between the Europeans and the American Indians?
4 What did the Europeans want?
5 What is the situation for American Indians these days?

**1** CD 3 12  **Listen and complete the place names.**

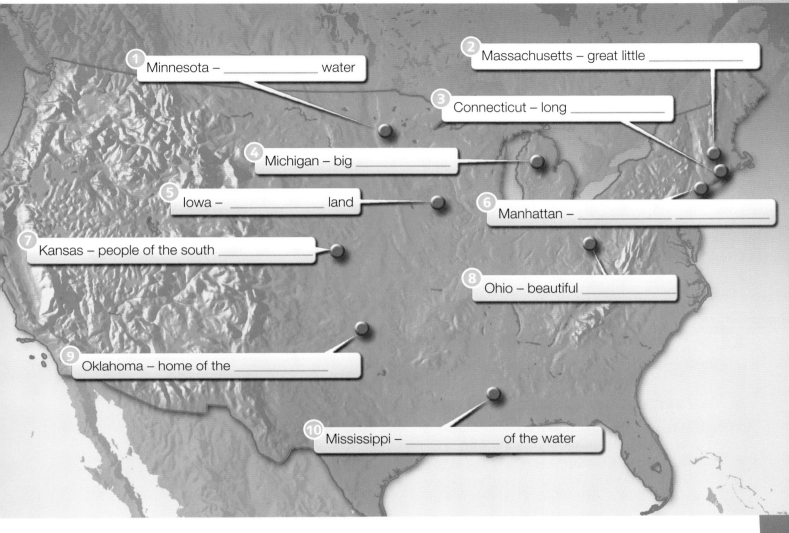

1 Minnesota – _____ water

2 Massachusetts – great little _____

3 Connecticut – long _____

4 Michigan – big _____

5 Iowa – _____ land

6 Manhattan – _____ _____

7 Kansas – people of the south _____

8 Ohio – beautiful _____

9 Oklahoma – home of the _____

10 Mississippi – _____ of the water

**2** Think of five places you and your partner know. How could American Indians describe these places?

London – place of many people
Paris – city with big tower
Rio de Janeiro – place of beautiful beaches

**3** Read your place names for your partner to guess.

City with beautiful opera house.

Is it Sydney?

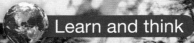

# GOLD

## 1 Write *t* (true) or *f* (false).

1 In some countries, people believe gold is good for your health, and they put it in snacks and drinks. ☐

2 Gold is sometimes used for building houses. People put it in the walls to keep their houses warm. ☐

3 Native American tribes believed eating gold could make you fly. ☐

4 There is a lot of gold in the seas and oceans. ☐

5 You can only find gold in water. ☐

6 All the gold that we have could be put in two big swimming pools. ☐

**Now turn your book upside down and check your answers.**

## 2 🔊 CD3 13 Read, listen, and find two reasons gold is so valuable.

Gold is expensive because …

## WHERE IS GOLD FOUND?

Gold is a precious metal. If you are very lucky, you could find a small gold nugget in a stream or even in your garden, but most gold is deep under the earth, and you need to build gold mines and use special machines to dig it out. This is difficult and is one of the reasons gold is so expensive. Gold is also expensive because it's very rare — that means there is not a lot of it.

There are gold mines in many countries. For many years, most gold came from South Africa, but now China is number one for gold production.

A gold mine in South Africa.

This is how people first looked for gold.

---

**1** **Look, read, and answer the questions. Think of other things that gold is used for.**

Gold is used for …

1 What is gold often used for?

2 Do you know any other precious metals? What are they used for?

# What is gold used for?

**Gold has many different uses. Here are some of them:**

## Money
Because gold is expensive, it is used as money. All over the world, people will always want to buy gold.

## Jewelry
60% of all the gold we have is made into jewelry. This is because gold is very soft and easy to work with. Gold is also used in jewelry because it's very beautiful.

## Electronics
All metals conduct electricity (meaning that electricity can move through them easily), but gold is better than most other metals. This means that gold is often used in machines like computers.

**2** **Project** **Make a trophy.**

**You need:**
- foam or cardboard coffee cups
- a small square box
- masking tape
- two pipe cleaners
- gold craft paint
- scissors
- paintbrush
- craft glue

1 Glue the bottoms of the two cups together.

2 Cover the box with masking tape.

3 When the glue between the cups has dried, wrap a piece of masking tape around the middle.

4 Insert a pipe cleaner into each side of one of the cups as trophy handles.

5 Cover the cups with masking tape.

6 Paint the tape on the cups and the box gold. Let them dry.

7 Use the glue to stick the bottom of the cup that does not have the pipe cleaner handles onto the box. Let the glue dry completely.

8 Think of someone to give the trophy to and tell them why.

# A Wanted Poster

**1** CD3 14   **Look at the poster and listen to the presentation. Make a note of three differences you hear.**

**WANTED**

## BETTY THE COYOTE

21 years old. 1.78 meters tall. Dark brown hair. Round face. Green eyes. Small nose. Bad teeth. Sometimes wears a red scarf and a black belt made of leather. Carries two pistols in brown holsters. Bring Betty the Coyote to any sheriff in Arizona. 500 dollars is waiting for you.

## Think about it

- Work with a friend. Think of a name for the person on your Wanted Poster.
- Draw a picture of the person. Think about what the person looks like and what clothes he or she wears.
- Draw a picture of the person on a big piece of paper. Color it in.
- Make notes about the person, where he or she is from, his or her clothes, other things he or she has (horse? pistols?).
- Think of how much the sheriff will pay for the person on your Wanted Poster.

## Prepare it

- On a piece of paper, write the text for your poster with your partner.
- Show it to your teacher to help you with the language.
- Write the text on your poster.

## Present it

- When you present your poster to the class, don't just read aloud the text. Say a little more.
  - ■ This is _____ .
  - ■ Be careful!
  - ■ There's a reward of _____ .

### i   Tips for presenters

When you give a presentation, you should speak a little bit louder than normal. Make sure everybody in your class can hear and understand what you are saying.

# Write a story

**1** **Complete the story with the correct sentences.**

a  "Everybody give me your money!" he shouted loudly.

b  "Who did this?" he shouted angrily.

c  "I'll get Hank Knife, and I'll put him behind bars!" he said.

d  "He's so mean, and he's very dangerous!" they said.

Hank Knife was a robber who lived in Sandhill. Everyone was afraid of him. (1) _____

It was a Friday. There were lots of people on the street. Suddenly they saw Hank Knife on his big, black horse. He stopped in front of the bank and went inside. (2) _____ The people gave him all their money.

But Sandhill had a new sheriff. He wasn't afraid of Hank Knife. (3) _____

When Hank Knife came back to his horse, there was a rope around the horse's legs. Hank was angry. (4) _____ Then he bent down to cut the rope. The sheriff jumped out from behind a barrel. He arrested Hank Knife.

**2** **Choose the best title for the story.**

Sandhill on a Friday

The big black horse

A lot of money

Bad luck for Hank Knife

**3** **Look at the questions and write a story with the title "Boris's last robbery."**

- Who is the main character of the story?
- What does he do?
- What happens?

 **Tips for writers**

Make your story interesting. Write three or four sentences to say what people said, shouted, or asked. Remember to use quotation marks.

**4** **In pairs, read your stories. How are they different?**

# 6 In Istanbul

Istanbul is one of the world's biggest and most beautiful cities. It is the only city in the world that is built on two continents – Europe and Asia. They are divided by a part of the sea that looks like a river: the Bosphorus Strait. Tourists love Istanbul because it offers the combination of a modern, Western lifestyle with fascinating Eastern traditions. In 2010, Istanbul was named the European Capital of Culture.

1. flag
2. sunglasses
3. earrings
4. carpet
5. basket
6. rings
7. cup and saucer
8. cushion
9. plate
10. soap
11. comb

**1** CD 3 15 **Listen and say the words. Check with your partner.**

**2** CD 3 16 **Read, listen, and answer the questions.**

1. What does Patrick want to buy and why?
2. Why doesn't Alex think that's a good idea?
3. Where are the children?
4. How does Phoebe know where they are?

**3** Choose a word. Draw it for your partner to guess. Can you think of any other things you can buy?  Is that a … ?

**1** **Read the text from a website for tourists. Then cover it up and complete the sentences.**

1 You should _____ comfortable shoes.

2 You should always _____ the name and address of your hotel on a piece of paper.

3 You shouldn't worry if you don't _____ Turkish. Many people speak English.

4 You should _____ a map when you walk around the city.

5 You shouldn't _____ pictures without asking.

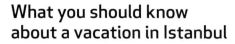
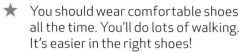

www.tipsfortourists.com

### What you should know about a vacation in Istanbul

★ You should wear comfortable shoes all the time. You'll do lots of walking. It's easier in the right shoes!

★ Make sure you know the name and the address of your hotel – write it on a piece of paper – Istanbul is a huge city. It's easy to get lost.

★ You shouldn't worry if you don't speak Turkish. Many Turkish people speak very good English and are very friendly and helpful. But why don't you learn a few words in Turkish? People will like that!

★ You should always take a map with you before you start walking around the city. And before you leave your hotel, you should make a plan of what you want to see.

★ You shouldn't take pictures without asking.

**2** CD 3 • 18  **Grammar focus**  **Listen and say the sentences.**

In the summer, you **shouldn't** go out without a hat. It can be very hot.

There are lots of cars. You **should** always be careful when crossing the road.

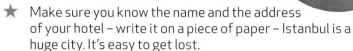

**3** **Make some fun rules for your classroom.**

You should bring an umbrella. It often rains here.

You shouldn't talk to the students here. They bite!

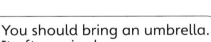

# Communication

**1** **Look at the picture and answer the questions.**

Mia and Olivia want to buy a present.
- What do you think they want to buy?
- Who is it for?

**2** CD3 19 **Read and listen to the dialog to check your answers.**

| | |
|---|---|
| **Mia** | This is the store. We'll definitely find Miss Saunders a present here. |
| **Olivia** | Let's get something nice. She's a great teacher. |
| **Mia** | Yes. I'm going to miss her next year. |
| **Olivia** | Look at those earrings. They're really cool. |
| **Mia** | They're OK … but I really like that ring over there. |
| **Olivia** | I'm not so sure. I prefer the earrings. |
| **Mia** | But they're not for you, they're for Miss Saunders. She'll like the ring best. |
| **Olivia** | She'll like the earrings more. |
| **Mia** | I don't agree, I think we should get the ring. |
| **Olivia** | I disagree, I think we should get the earrings! |
| **Mia** | OK, let's see how much they cost. Can you read the prices? |
| **Olivia** | Let me see. Um, the earrings are … $350! |
| **Mia** | What! |

| | |
|---|---|
| **Olivia** | And the ring's … $3,000! |
| **Mia** | OK, I think we should go to another store! |
| **Olivia** | I agree! |
| **Mia** | Come on! |

**3** **Work in pairs.**

a Practice the dialog.

b Imagine you want to buy someone a present. Decide on:
- who it is for
- why you want to buy a present
- two things you could get

c Use your ideas to make up your own new dialog.

d Act out your dialog for the class.

**Disagreeing**
They're / It's OK but …
I'm not so sure.
I don't agree.
I disagree.

**1** **Read and listen to the dialogs. Match them with the pictures.**

☐ **A** Could I see that ring over there, please?
**B** Of course.

☐ **A** Do you mind if I open this book?
**B** Not at all.

☐ **A** Do you mind if I try on this jacket?
**B** Not at all.

☐ **A** Could I buy some stamps for these postcards, please?
**B** Of course.

 **2** Grammar focus **Listen and say the questions and answers.**

**Could I** try on that T-shirt over there? **Of course.**
**Do you mind if I** close the door? **Not at all.**

**3** **Play tourist and sales clerk in a souvenir shop. Then swap roles.**

- Could you show me / tell me / give me … ?
- Could I see/have … ?
- Do you mind if I try this on / look at the … ?

**1** Look at the pictures. What do you think happens to Phoebe in the story?

**2** CD 3 24 Read and listen to the story to check your answers.

# Lost in the city

Phoebe bought a little guidebook about Istanbul from the tourist office. The Time Travelers sat down to read it. "Let's go sightseeing!" said Phoebe. She was so excited. The pictures in her book were wonderful. "This city's great!" Patrick said. "Let's go!" They made a list of all the sights they wanted to see. "We should go by subway," said Phoebe. "This city's so big, we can't walk all day."

The closest subway station was called Taksim. It was full of people, and it was hard for the Travelers to move fast. "There's the train! Hurry!" Patrick shouted. Patrick and Alex pushed through the crowd and jumped onto the train. Phoebe wasn't fast enough. The doors closed before she could get in! She didn't know what to do. "Stop!" she shouted, but that didn't help.

Alex and Patrick talked about what to do. How would they find Phoebe in a city of more than 12 million people? "Let's go and see all the sights we wanted to see," Patrick said. "Phoebe knows what they are. I'm sure we'll find her at one of them!" The boys spent six hours in Istanbul. They visited the Blue Mosque with its beautiful blue tiles. They visited the Bosphorus Bridge and the Spice Market, but they didn't find Phoebe. They were really worried.

"Can I help you?" a voice said. "I'm Ali." Ali was about the same age as them, and he was very friendly. Alex and Patrick told him what had happened. "Hmm. You lost your friend at the subway station in Taksim. She's probably waiting for you there!" he said. "Of course!" Alex and Patrick shouted. "Let's go back to Taksim!"

Sure enough, when the three boys arrived at Taksim, they found Phoebe waiting on the platform where they had last seen her.

"I'm so sorry!" Patrick said. "It wasn't very smart to get on the train without you!" Phoebe laughed. "I'm so happy we're together again. So happy! But what did you do all day?" The boys told her about all the beautiful places. "I'd love to see them, too!" Phoebe said. "We can go and see them tomorrow!" said Ali. "That's a great idea," said Phoebe, "but we can't stay!" "Why not?" asked Ali. "Istanbul is beautiful!" "I know," Phoebe said sadly. She was looking up toward the escalator where there was a yellow glow.

Ali was sad about saying goodbye. He saw his three new friends going up the escalator. They waved at him. Then they slowly moved into the light and were gone in a flash.

**3** **Correct the mistakes in the sentences.**

1 Phoebe, Alex, and Patrick looked at a book with some pictures of the subway.

2 They decided to travel around the city by bus.

3 Alex and Patrick went to see some sights. They wanted to find Ali, their friend.

4 They went back to Taksim with a Turkish girl.

5 When they arrived in Taksim, they couldn't find Phoebe.

6 Ali wanted to show Phoebe the city the next day, but she didn't like Istanbul.

**4** **Think!** **Look at the picture and answer the questions with the phrases in the box.**

in front of   behind   to the left   to the right

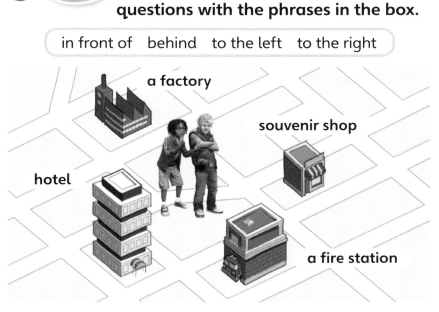

a factory

souvenir shop

hotel

a fire station

Where is the
• hotel? • factory? • souvenir shop? • fire station?

Alex and Patrick now turn to face the left. Now where are the buildings?

**1**  **Match the flags with the countries. Listen and check.**

1 India 2 Indonesia 3 Finland
4 China 5 Japan 6 U.S.A.
7 Mexico 8 Germany

**2** **Read about the things these countries make.**

Would you be surprised to learn that you have things from all over the world? Take a look around your room. Those sneakers on the floor (the ones your parents are always asking you to put away) are made in Indonesia on the other side of the world. Your jeans and T-shirt (also a mess on the floor) come from Mexico or India, on completely opposite sides of the world.

Now find your cell phone. You can't. Look under the bed. There it is! What does that say? "Made in Finland." And your computer, well, that came all the way from China.

Your mom's home from work. You can hear her car stopping outside the house. That new car that she spends all Sunday cleaning was made in Germany and then put on a ship and brought all the way over here.

Your homework is done – well, most of it is. You're tired, and you need to relax. You lie on your bed, and you decide to turn on the TV, which came all the way from Japan. There's a French movie on. You're too tired to read the subtitles, so you turn over and watch an American police series. Who needs to travel the world? It's all here in your home.

**3** **Read again and choose the best title for it. Write it above the text.**

- The world in your room.
- Why is your room always such a mess?
- Made in China.

**4** **Work in pairs. Make a list of the things in your home that are made in your country.**

> pencils
> lamp
> chair

**5** **Write your ideas on the board and make a class list.**

**1** CD 3 27  **Listen and draw lines from the countries to the food.**

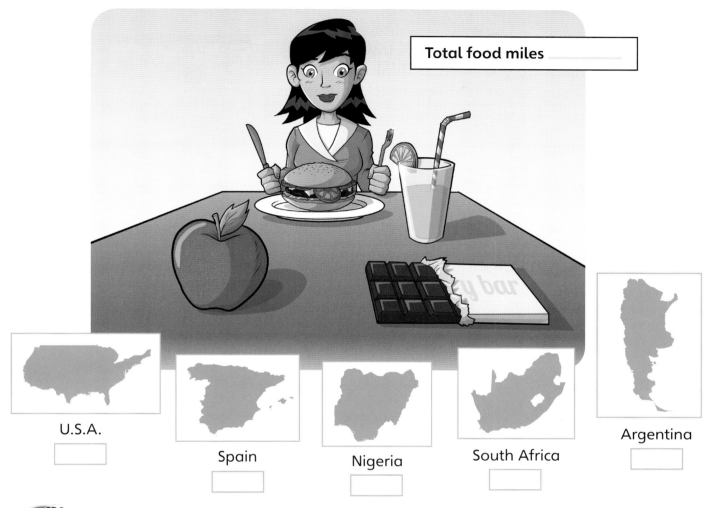

Total food miles

U.S.A.

Spain

Nigeria

South Africa

Argentina

**2** CD 3 28  **How many kilometers has the food traveled? Listen again and write the numbers in the boxes. What is the total?**

**3** **Discuss the questions in small groups.**

1   What food that you eat comes from other countries?

2   What food that you eat definitely comes from your country?

3   Is it a good or a bad thing to eat food that travels a long way? Why?

**4** **Find out where all the food for your breakfast comes from and how far it has to travel. Write a short text.**

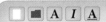

For breakfast today I had a bowl of cereal with milk and a banana. The cereal came from the U.S.A. The banana came from Brazil, but the milk came from my own country.

# Town Planning

**1** CD 3 29 **Imagine you are planning a new town. What kinds of things do you need to think about? Read and listen to the text and check your ideas.**

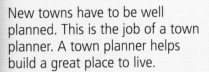

## Town Planning

New towns have to be well planned. This is the job of a town planner. A town planner helps build a great place to live.

Town planners have to think about many things. Should people live in apartment buildings or smaller buildings? How will people get to work? Should there be a subway system, buses, and trains?

Town planners also have to think about cars. Where will people park? How big do the roads need to be?

Planners make sure that different parts of the town have parks, playgrounds, and swimming pools for adults and children to enjoy. They need to think about where to put stores and supermarkets and about schools, libraries, and hospitals.

Town planners also have to think about what kinds of jobs people can do in the new town. There will be many jobs in stations, restaurants, schools, stores, and hospitals. It's important that people live close to where they work. As you can see, the job of a town planner is not an easy one. There are many things to think about, and it is important that they get it all right so that people are happy to live in the town.

**2** **We need lots of different places in a town, and we need lots of people to work in those places. Where do these people work? Create a chart.**

| sports center | restaurant | hospital | train station | school | store |
|---|---|---|---|---|---|
| | | | | | |

**3** **How many more different places in a town can you think of?**

**1** Town planners think about what places towns need and the best location for them. What places do you think are important for these people? Choose three places for each person.

**2** What four places are the most important for you in your town/area?

The … is the most …

**3** Project  Plan a town.

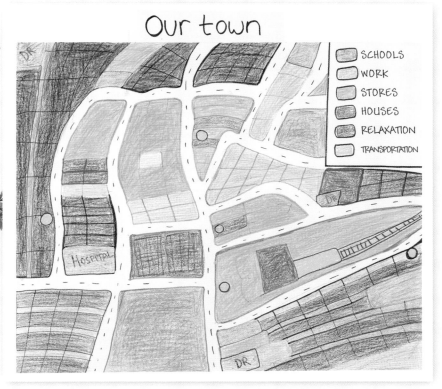

Our town

SCHOOLS
WORK
STORES
HOUSES
RELAXATION
TRANSPORTATION

1 Make a simple map of your town/area.

2 Color-code the different places – schools, hospitals and doctors, places people shop, relax, work, live, get transportation from.

3 What do you notice about where the different places are?

4 Think of three changes or new places that would improve your area.

# At a clothes store

**1** **Work in pairs.
Choose a role card.**

**Student A**

You are the customer.

You want to buy some clothes. Think about the following:

- what you would like to buy
- how much the items cost
- whether they have the item in another color or another size
- if you can try it on
- what the item is made of

**Student B**

You are a sales clerk.

You ask/tell the customer:

- what they would like to buy
- how much the items are
- if you have the item in another size and color
- where they can try the item on
- what the item is made of

**2** **Act out your dialog.**

## Useful language

**Student A**

I'm looking for …
How much is/are … ?
Could you show me a different … ?
Do you have it in another … ?
Do you mind if I … ? / Can I … ?
What is it … ?

**Student B**

I can show you …
It's/They're …
Here we have …
No problem.
I'll check if …
Come this way.
It's made of …

# A leaflet giving advice

**1** Gavin is a new member of the basketball team. The trainer has written up some rules for him. Write *should* or *shouldn't*.

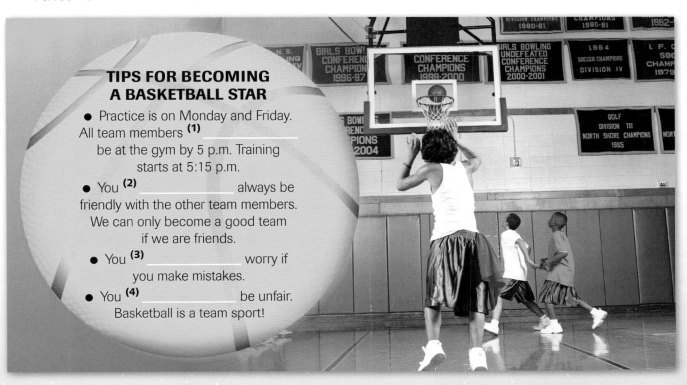

**TIPS FOR BECOMING A BASKETBALL STAR**

- Practice is on Monday and Friday. All team members **(1)** _____ be at the gym by 5 p.m. Training starts at 5:15 p.m.
- You **(2)** _____ always be friendly with the other team members. We can only become a good team if we are friends.
- You **(3)** _____ worry if you make mistakes.
- You **(4)** _____ be unfair. Basketball is a team sport!

**2** Add the missing word to each tip.

You ∧ always help other players if they have a problem.

When another player makes a mistake, you ∧ laugh.

You ∧ do a lot of training.

You ∧ forget that basketball is a team sport.

 **Tips for writers**

**Before you start writing, take time to think. Make notes.**

Think about:
- places they should visit.
- places they shouldn't visit.
- the weather and what clothes they should wear.
- how much money they should bring and what they should buy.
- where they should stay.
- how long they should stay.

**3** Write a leaflet giving advice to a visitor to your town.

# 7 The story teller

William Shakespeare (1564–1616) is one of the world's most famous writers. He lived in England all his life and wrote lots of plays and poems. You can see his plays today in theaters all over the world. One of his most famous plays is *Romeo and Juliet*. It's a sad story about a boy and a girl who are in love, but their families are enemies.

1 audience
2 candles
3 mask
4 lute
5 actor
6 wig
7 costume
8 tights

**1** CD 3 30    **Listen and say the words. Check with your partner.**

**2** CD 3 31    **Read, listen, and complete the sentences.**

1   Alex thinks the theater is _____ .

2   Mrs. Butler showed them pictures of _____ and the Globe _____ .

3   The audience _____ the play.

4   Phoebe thinks the play is _____ .

**3**   **Choose a word. Describe it for your partner to guess.**

They are in movies and plays.

**1**  CD 3 32 **Read and listen to the dialog. Who brings each item? Write the names below the items.**

**Paul** What do we need for the play?

**Lisa** We need costumes, two wigs, a necklace and a bracelet for the queen, and a sword for the king. I'll bring the costumes.

**Daisy** I'll bring a blond wig from my grandmother.

**Harry** I think we have a black wig at home. I'll ask my mom if I can have it.

**Lisa** Great. What about the necklace and the bracelet?

**Adam** I'll check at home. I'm sure my sister has lots of them.

**Lisa** Excellent. What about a sword?

**Lily** I'll make one.

**Paul** I'll bring some hats. We have lots of old ones at home.

**Lisa** Great. Thank you all. See you tomorrow at three.

**2** CD 3 33 **Grammar focus** **Listen and say the sentences.**

> **I'll ask** my sister to give us a bracelet.
> **I'll get** my mom to make us a costume.
> **We'll get** some sandwiches from the store.

**3** **Work with your partner. How can you help them? Then swap roles.**

- I'm thirsty.
- I can't do my homework.
- This bag is very heavy.

- I'm hungry.
- It's cold in here.
- I can't find my camera.

> I'm thirsty.

> I'll get you a glass of orange juice.

**1** CD 3 34 **Listen and correct the mistakes. Then sing the song.**

I'll buy you a ~~parrot~~, (1) _____
I'll buy you a nice hat,
I'll buy you a bracelet,
I'll buy you a car. (2) _____

I really don't believe you,
When you promise me these things,
You'll never buy me necklaces,
You'll never buy me rings.

I'll write you a comic book, (3) _____
I'll tell you a secret,
I'll sing you a song,
I'll build you a house. (4) _____

I really don't believe you,
When you promise me these things,
You'll never write me poems,
You'll never buy me rings.

I'll take you to the circus, (5) _____
I'll take you to the sea, (6) _____
I'll take you to a show,
I'll do it all for you.

I really don't believe you,
When you promise me these things,
You'll never take me to a show,
You'll never buy me rings.

### All about music: **Duets**

When two people sing a song together, it is called a duet. Often the singers are a man and a woman, and the songs are romantic ballads. These songs can be about happy times, but they are usually about when things go wrong.

**What I think**
- It's great.
- It's OK.
- I don't really like it.

 **2** CD 3 36 **Listen and say the dialog.**

**Olive** Let's go to the Shakespeare theater!
**George** Isn't it a little expensive, dear?
**Olive** Yes, but I promise – you'll love it, George!
**George** Um … of course I will, Olive.

**1** **What are the actors doing? Match the pictures with the sentences.**

1 He's just read some good news.
2 He's just heard some bad news.
3 He's just cut his finger.

4 She's just dropped a book on her foot.
5 She's just gotten up.
6 She's just had a fright.

**2** CD 3 40 **Grammar focus** **Listen and say the sentences.**

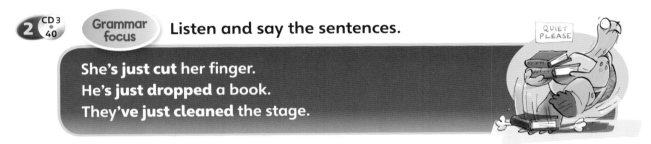

She's **just cut** her finger.
He's **just dropped** a book.
They've **just cleaned** the stage.

QUIET PLEASE

**3** **Play the game. Mime and say.**

Finished.

You've just eaten an apple.

That's right.

**1** Go through the text quickly and find answers to the questions.

a How do the children think Shakespeare should change the end of his play?

b What does the audience think of the new end to the play?

**2** (CD 4 02) Read and listen to the story to check your answers.

# *Helping Shakespeare*

"Let's go and talk to Shakespeare," said Phoebe, "I feel sorry for him." "How can we help him?" answered Alex. "I have an idea," Phoebe said. The friends climbed up onto the stage. Shakespeare was sitting on a big box. The children said hello. "I don't know what to do," Shakespeare said. "The audience didn't like my play. They shouted and threw eggs and vegetables onto the stage." "Maybe we can help you," said Phoebe. "I don't see how you can do that," Shakespeare answered sadly.

Suddenly they heard shouting. "Where is he? We want our money back!" Two men with big sticks were in the theater looking for Shakespeare. They looked very angry. "Stand at the edge of the stage," said Patrick. "Hurry, they're coming! When they're close, wave your arms in the air." Shakespeare stood next to the box at the edge of the stage. Patrick picked up an actor's sword,

and he hid behind the box with Alex. When the two men saw Shakespeare, they ran up to him shouting, "Give us our money back!"

The men ran toward Shakespeare. When they were very close, he waved his hands, and Patrick tripped them with the sword. With a loud crash they fell off the stage. "Run, or I'll get you with my sword," Patrick shouted. The men ran away. They were very scared. Shakespeare was happy. "Thank you, you've just saved my life!" he said. "Please come to my house and have dinner with me."

At Shakespeare's house the children and Shakespeare talked about *Romeo and Juliet*. "Maybe the audience didn't like the happy ending," Phoebe said. "Why don't you rewrite the ending so that they both die? Maybe the audience will like that ending better." Right then, they heard voices outside.

Shakespeare opened the door. It was the men from the theater with some of their friends. They looked very angry. "That's him," said one of the men pointing at Patrick. "He's the one who had the sword." They all started walking toward Patrick. "Stop!" shouted Shakespeare. "Leave the boy alone, or you will never know the new ending of my play." "New ending?" said one of the men. "What happens?" "Come and see," said Shakespeare. "There are free tickets for all of you."

The Time Travelers watched from the side of the stage. The audience was enjoying the play, and Shakespeare was very happy. At the end, the audience clapped. Shakespeare looked at the kids and waved his hand for them to join him on the stage. As they walked up to it, they saw the yellow glow in front of them. They stepped through and were gone in a flash.

---

**3** **Put the sentences in order.**

☐ Alex and Patrick save Shakespeare from the two men.

☐ Some angry men arrive at Shakespeare's house.

☐ Shakespeare invites the three friends for dinner.

☐ The three friends are in a theater.

☐ The three friends talk to Shakespeare.

☐ Shakespeare offers some free tickets to the men.

☐ The audience does not like the ending of the play.

☐ Two men want their money back.

☐ The audience likes the ending of the play.

**4**   **Think!** **Match the differences between Shakespeare's Globe and theaters now. Can you think of another difference?**

| Shakespeare's Globe | | Theaters now | |
|---|---|---|---|
| 1 | There were candles to light the stage. | a | Everyone sits down. |
| 2 | The actors were all men. | b | Most theaters are inside. |
| 3 | Most of the audience stood up. | c | There are electric lights. |
| 4 | If the play was bad, people threw fruit. | d | Actors can be men or women. |
| 5 | Many theaters did not have a roof. | e | If they do not like the play, people leave. |

**1** Look at the book covers. Work with your partner and guess why the books are special.

Was it written by a child?

Does it only have one sentence?

Was it the first book ever printed?

Is it the shortest book in the world?

**2** (CD4 03) Listen and check your answers. Why are these books special?

*Gadsby* is special because …

**3** (CD4 04) Listen again and answer the questions.

1 How many words are in *Gadsby*? _____

2 How many paintings are in *Birds of America*? _____

3 How much did a copy of *Birds of America* sell for? _____

4 When was the collection of fairy tales first published? _____

5 Into how many languages was *The Very Hungry Caterpillar* translated? _____

**4** Read about 50-word stories and think about the questions.

Can you write a story using exactly 50 words? Look at this example. It tells the story of Shakespeare's *Romeo and Juliet*. There is only one problem. It has five words too many. Can you make it exactly 50 words long?

Romeo and Juliet fall in love. Their families are great enemies – so they decide to get married in secret. Before this, Juliet pretends to die to avoid marrying a man she doesn't like very much. Romeo thinks she is dead and so he kills himself. Juliet wakes up, sees Romeo's dead body, and kills herself.

**5** **Think!** Think of a story you know well and tell it in 50 words. If you want, you can be like Ernest Vincent Wright and not use any word with an *e* in it.

**1** **Look at the pictures and answer the questions.**

1 What are the three men doing?

2 What does the man want to do with the cow?

**2** CD 4 05 **Read, listen, and check your answers.**

## A SMART WOMAN

Marlowe was the richest man in the village. One evening, three men knocked at his door. They were tired and wanted a bed for the night. "You can sleep in the stable," said Marlowe, "and my servant will bring you some soup." The strangers said thank you and went to the stable. In the middle of the night, one of the men got up quietly. He took a rope and tied it around a cow's neck. He led the cow into a forest and tied it to a tree. "I'll get the cow in the morning and sell her in the market," he thought.

Next morning, the servant went to milk the cows. When he saw that one cow was missing, he went to tell Marlowe. Marlowe went to the stable. "Did you steal one of my cows?" he asked. "Of course not," the three men answered. "We were asleep all night."

Marlowe told his wife about the cow. "I'm sure that one of the three men stole the cow." She said, "I have a plan."

They went to the stable, and she said to the men, "We have a very smart dog called Barney. He will show us who stole the cow. Go into the room where Barney is and stroke him. When the thief strokes Barney's fur, the dog will bark."

The first man went into the room. The dog didn't make a sound. The second man went in. The dog didn't make a sound. Finally the third man went in. The dog still didn't make a sound. "Did you all stroke the dog's fur?" asked the woman. "Yes," they said. Then Marlowe's wife asked to smell the hand that each man used to stroke the dog. She smelled them in turn. When she got to the third man, she said, "You are the thief. Our dog Barney is very smelly. Your friends' hands smell of Barney. Your hand doesn't. You didn't stroke Barney's fur because you were afraid that Barney would bark. Now tell us where the cow is."

**3** **Match the sentence halves to make the summary.**

| | | | |
|---|---|---|---|
| 1 | Three men were looking | a | in the market the next day. |
| 2 | Marlowe told them to sleep in the stable | b | smell of Barney. |
| 3 | In the middle of the night, one of the men | c | and gave them some soup. |
| 4 | He wanted to sell it | d | the dog's fur. |
| 5 | In the morning, one of the servants | e | who the thief was. |
| 6 | The farmer told his wife, who | f | had a plan. |
| 7 | The three men had to stroke | g | for a place to stay overnight. |
| 8 | The thief's hand didn't | h | saw that a cow was missing. |
| 9 | So the farmer's wife knew | i | took Marlowe's cow into a forest. |

# Poetry

**1** **Read the text below and find out about poetry.**

Poetry has a long history. Thousands of years ago, when most people could not read or write, poets told stories about the adventures of men and women in the form of poems. Poetry is still popular today, and what's so great about it is that anyone can write it. Poems can be about people, objects, animals, the weather, and feelings. In fact, they can be about anything. Poems often rhyme, but they don't have to.

**2** **Read the three poems. Say which you like best and why.**

*The first example is by the American poet Jack Prelutsky.*

*The second poem is by Roger McGough, an English poet.*

## My Mother Makes Me Chicken

My mother makes me chicken,
her chicken makes me cough.
I wish that when she made it,
she took the feathers off.

## Fame

The best thing
about being famous

is when you walk
down the street

and people turn round
to look at you

and bump into things.

*The last example is by Shel Silverstein, who began writing when he was 12 years old. Shel Silverstein also wrote plays and music for movies.*

## Spaghetti

Spaghetti, spaghetti, all over the place,
Up to my elbows – up to my face,
Over the carpet and under the chairs,
Into the hammock and wound round the stairs,
Filling the bathtub and covering the desk,
Making the sofa a mad mushy mess.

The party is ruined, I'm terribly worried,
The guests have all left (unless they're all buried).
I told them, "Bring presents." I said, "Throw confetti."
I guess they heard wrong
'Cause they all threw spaghetti!

### 1 Discuss in groups.

1 Do you ever read poetry?

2 Do you know the names of poets in your country?

3 Do you know any poems by heart?

### 2 Project Write poetry.

1 Read the examples of different kinds of poems.

## The story I'm going to write
by Jorge Xirau (11)

There is a castle,
there are dragons,
there is a black knight,
there is a queen,
and there are lots of fights
in the story I'm going to write.

**What to do:**
Use the following
model for your poem.

There is/are … ,
there is/are … ,
there is/are … ,
there is/are … ,
and there is/are …
in the story I'm going
to write.

## Acrostic
by Carlos Vallejo (11)

**C**hicken loving
**A**ngry (sometimes)
**R**uns fast
**L**ucky
**O**ne sister
**S**uper soccer player!

**What to do:** Choose a
word (a person, a place
name, an animal, a school
subject … ). Write the
letters of the word in a
vertical line. Then write a
word or a phrase beginning
with the letter of each line.
Try to describe the thing
that you have chosen.

## Color poem
by Ana Romero (12)

White is the car
that my mom drives.

White are the flowers
in our garden.

White is the pen
that I use.

White is the board
in our classroom.

**What to do:**
Choose a color.
Write about
things that are
that color. Try
to think of lots
of different and
interesting things.

### 3 Choose a kind of poem and write one.

### 4 Stick your poems on the wall in your classroom. Read as many poems as possible. Talk about the poems you like.

I like your poem because …

The words I like in your poem are …

Your poem is really great.

# Class survey

 **1** **CD 4 06** **Listen to the presentation on books and look at the bar chart. Find two differences.**

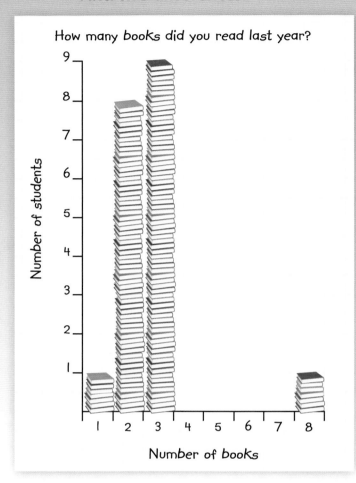

How many *books* did you read last year?

Number of students

Number of books

## Think about it

- Who is your favorite writer?
- What is your favorite book?
- Is there a book you didn't like at all?
- What book are you reading right now?
- What was the last book you read?
- Where do you read? In your room? In the living room? Somewhere outside?
- How many hours do you read per week?
- How many books did you read last year?

## Prepare it

- Choose eight interviewers, one for each question.
- The interviewers walk around the class and ask everyone their question.
- The interviewers write down their classmates' answers.

## Present it

- In groups, use the interviewers' notes to prepare a large bar chart for each question.
- Look at the example in Activity 1.
- Show the bar chart to the class and explain it.

 **2** **CD 4 07** **Match the sentence halves. Listen again and check.**

| | | | |
|---|---|---|---|
| 1 | Here are | a | read three books. |
| 2 | Let me explain | b | a few things. |
| 3 | As you can see | c | our results. |
| 4 | A total of nine students | d | for listening. |
| 5 | Thank you | e | from the bar graph. |

 **Tips for presenters**

Take your time explaining the bar chart. Make sure your classmates understand what each of the two lines mean. Write in big letters "Number of students" / "Number of books."

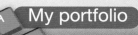 
# A biography

**1 Complete the biography of William Shakespeare with the phrases from the box.**

> at the age of 18   he spent the rest of his life
> He died in 1616   He was born in   In 1598
> Between 1585 and 1592

Many people consider William Shakespeare to be the greatest writer in the English language. However, not a lot is known about his life.
(1)_____ 1564 in Stratford-upon-Avon in England. He was the third of seven children for his parents, John and Mary. He went to a good school, and (2)_____
he married Anne Hathaway. She was eight years older than him. They had three children.

(3)_____, he started a successful theater company in London where he wrote, produced, and acted in his plays.

(4)_____, his company moved to the famous Globe theater. In 1603, King James I gave Shakespeare's company royal support. In 1610, Shakespeare retired from the theater, and (5)_____ in Stratford-upon-Avon. (6)_____ at the age of 52.

**2 Answer the questions.**

1 How many brothers and sisters did Shakespeare have?

2 In what year did he get married?

3 How old was Anne when they married?

4 How old was Shakespeare when he returned to Stratford?

**3 Complete the sentences so that they are true about you.**

> At the age of _____ I _____
> .
> I was born _____ .
> In 20____
> I _____ .
> Between 20____ and 20____
> I _____
> _____
> _____
> _____ .

**i 🔍 Tips for writers**

When you write a biography, make sure you put the facts in order. In a story, there is always a beginning, a middle, and an end. In a story about a person's life, this is the same.

**4 Research a person you like and write a short biography of him or her. Use time phrases.**

# 8 Museum of the future

When we go to a museum, we see things from the past, and we learn about how people used to live. When you see a train or a plane in a museum, they look very different from the planes and trains of today. What will museums of the future show? They will show the planes and trains that we think are modern now. To visitors in the future, these things will look old!

1) businessman
2) janitor
3) engineer
4) dentist
5) businesswoman
6) artist
7) farmer
8) mechanic
9) computer programmer

**1** CD4 08 **Listen and say the words. Check with your partner.**

**2** CD4 09 **Read, listen, and answer the questions.**

1 What did Phoebe's grandpa do?
2 Why is the museum strange?
3 What year is it?
4 How is the world different?

**3** **Choose a word. Describe it for your partner to guess.**

He works with animals.

**1** CD 4
10

**Listen to the ad. Color the buttons.**

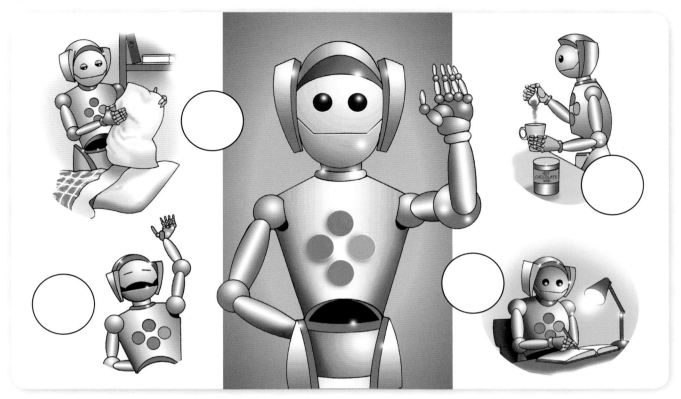

**2** CD 4
11

**Grammar focus**  **Listen and say the sentences.**

> **If** you**'re** thirsty, the robot **will** make you a nice cup of hot chocolate.
> **If** you**'re** tired, it**'ll** do your homework.
> **If** you**'re** bored, it**'ll** sing you a song.

**3** **Play the robot game with a partner.**

If you're hungry, I'll make you a sandwich.

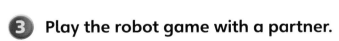

## Communication

**1** **Look at the picture and answer the question.**

What do you think Mia, Charlie, and Josh are doing?

**2** CD 4 • 12 **Read and listen to the dialog to check your answer.**

| | |
|---|---|
| **Mia** | I'm bored. Let's watch TV. |
| **Josh** | Yeah, I'm bored, too. Come on, Charlie. Why don't we turn the TV on? |
| **Charlie** | No, the math test is tomorrow, so let's do some review. That's what we're here for. |
| **Josh** | I hate math! |
| **Mia** | Me, too. Why do we have to learn math? |
| **Josh** | I don't know. We never use it in real life. |
| **Charlie** | I thought you wanted to be an engineer. |
| **Josh** | Yes, I do, just like my dad. |
| **Charlie** | You'll never be an engineer if you don't know any math. |
| **Josh** | Really? |
| **Charlie** | Yes, engineers work with numbers all the time. |
| **Mia** | Well, what about me? |
| **Charlie** | What do you want to be? |
| **Mia** | I want to be a rich businesswoman. |
| **Charlie** | Well, then you definitely need to be good at math. |
| **Mia** | Why? |
| **Charlie** | How will you count all your money if you can't do math? |
| **Mia** | You're right. Come on, Josh, let's do some review! |

**3** **Work in pairs.**

a Practice the dialog.

b You are studying for a test. Decide:
- what subject the test is on.
- what jobs you want to do.
- why that subject is important for the jobs.

c Use your ideas to make up your own dialog.

d Act out your dialog for the class.

**?** **What to say**

**Making suggestions**
Let's …
Why don't we … ?

**1** **Read and listen to the dialog. What will Pete do on Sunday?**

**Rich** What can we do on Sunday?

**Pete** Let me think. Oh, I know. We can build a tree house.

**Rich** But what if it rains?

**Pete** Then we'll go to my room and listen to music.

**Rich** But what if I don't like your music?

**Pete** Then we'll play computer games.

**Rich** But what if your computer doesn't work?

**Pete** Then we'll have some ice cream!

**Rich** But what if it's too cold for ice cream?

**Pete** Then we'll make some tomato soup.

**Rich** But what if you don't have any tomatoes at home?

**Pete** Then we'll make some hot chocolate.

**Rich** But what if I don't want any hot chocolate?

**Pete** Oh, sorry, I don't have any time on Sunday.

**Rich** Why's that?

**Pete** Because … if it's sunny, I'll build a tree house. If it rains, I'll listen to …

 **2**  **Grammar focus** **Listen and say the dialogs.**

**Rich** Let's go to the movies.

**Pete** But **what if** the movie isn't good?

**Rich** Then we'll watch a soccer game.

**Rich** Let's go to the museum.

**Pete** But **what if** it's closed?

**Rich** Then we'll go shopping.

**3** **Read the examples and play the *But what if … ?* game.**

> Let's ride our bikes.　Let's play soccer.　　Let's take a walk.
> Let's go to the zoo.　Let's sing a song.　　Let's help Dad.

Let's ride our bikes.　　But what if it rains?

We'll get a little wet.　　But what if we catch a cold?

We'll miss a few days of school.

But what if we miss an important test … ?

**1** Work in pairs. Look at the pictures and the title of the story.

a   Write down words that come to your mind.       b   Make a story out of your words.

**2** CD4 17   Read and listen to the story to find out if it is similar to or different from your story.

# The trouble with Orangehead XR-97

The children walked around the museum. There were some sports cars and motorcycles at the end of it. "Amazing!" Alex thought. "People don't use cars and motorcycles anymore!" "Boring," said Patrick, "I'm going." "Where?" shouted Phoebe. Patrick pointed at a door with a *Don't enter* sign on it. "Let's open that door," he said. "Patrick, no!" said Phoebe.

Patrick didn't listen. He went into the room. Alex and Phoebe followed him. Inside sat a big robot with an orange head. It was at a computer with its back to the children. "Tomorrow I'll be master of the world!" laughed the robot. The children were scared. "What can we do?" Patrick whispered. "Let's get out of here," said Phoebe.

They left the room and heard a sound coming from a submarine. "Help! Help me!" "What's that?" Patrick asked. There

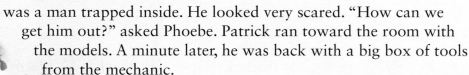

was a man trapped inside. He looked very scared. "How can we get him out?" asked Phoebe. Patrick ran toward the room with the models. A minute later, he was back with a big box of tools from the mechanic.

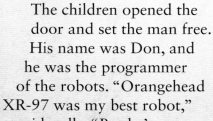

The children opened the door and set the man free. His name was Don, and he was the programmer of the robots. "Orangehead XR-97 was my best robot," Don said sadly. "But he's dangerous. He locked me in the submarine. He wants to take over the world. If we don't stop him, he will destroy everyone." The children were very worried. "What can we do?" asked Alex.

Don had an idea, "Every morning from 6:55 to 7 o'clock, all the robots shut down for five minutes to charge their batteries. That's our only chance. But now we have to hide. Hurry!"

"Hide? Where?" said Patrick. "Get on a motorcycle or in a car. But don't move," said Don. Don climbed back into the submarine. When the robots came to clean the room, they saw two boys in the sports car and a girl on the motorcycle, but they thought they were wax models.

The next morning at 6:55, Don and the children entered the computer room. It was full of very quiet robots, including Orangehead XR-97. Don switched on the computer and worked very quickly. At seven o'clock there was a loud noise. The Time Travelers saw flames and smoke coming out of Orangehead XR-97. "I destroyed it!" Don said.

He turned around to thank the children and saw a bright glowing yellow light. The children waved goodbye and stepped into the light. They were gone in a flash.

**3** **Complete the sentences. You can use 1, 2, 3, or 4 words.**

1  The kids saw a door with a *Don't enter* sign, but _____.
2  They found out that the robot _____ wanted to take over the world.
3  They went to a room and found a man _____.
4  He told them that the robot with the orange head was his best robot, but _____.
5  The robots _____ to recharge their batteries.
6  Don Singleton didn't like it, but he had to _____.

**4** ( Think! ) **Work in groups. Read and answer.**

1  Two fathers and two sons were making robots. Each of them made one robot. So why did they only have three robots when they finished?
2  A scientist made a robot that looked like a horse. He rode to town on Sunday, stayed two days, and left town on Sunday. How did he do it?

**1 Discuss in pairs.**

Look at the list of unusual jobs. One of them is not real. Which one do you think it is? What do you think the other jobs involve?

I think the fruit cleaner is not a real job.

fruit cleaner

pet detective

ostrich babysitter

elephant dancer

**2**  **Listen and check your answers.**

**3**  **Listen again. Write *t* (true) or *f* (false). Correct the false ones.**

1   Pet food testers don't usually eat the food. ☐
2   Fruit cleaners work in supermarkets. ☐
3   There is a movie about a pet detective. ☐
4   Taking care of ostriches is a very busy job. ☐
5   Golf ball divers give the balls back to the golfers. ☐

pet food tester

**4 Work in pairs. Think of (or make up) an unusual job. Think of what the job involves and give the job a name.**

**5 Tell the class about your unusual job and decide which is the best one.**

**6 Write a short text about your unusual job.**

golf ball diver

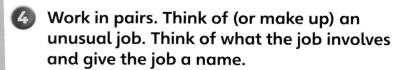

Leaf cleaners clean leaves in gardens to make them look nice …

**1** Discuss in pairs.

Think about firefighters. What do they do?
Are they usually men or women?

> Firefighters help …

**2** Read the interview with a firefighter. Does she like her job?

**1**

My grandfather and my uncle were both firefighters, so it's a job I knew quite a lot about. When I was a little girl, I always wanted to be one, but when I grew up, I stopped thinking about it and looked for other jobs.

**2**

For a while I worked in a circus! That was fun. And then I was a gym teacher for a few years.

**3**

One day, I took some of the schoolchildren on a trip to the fire station. I was amazed at how excited I got, and I knew I had to try to do this job. A year later I was a firefighter.

**4**

Well, he's also a firefighter, so he can't really complain. We work at different fire stations, so we don't see each other at work very often – only when there's a really big fire.

**5**

Lots of things. I love working at different times of the day. When I was a teacher, I always worked from 9 a.m. until 3:30 p.m. As a firefighter, I work at lots of different times. It makes the job interesting. I also like the friends I have at the fire station.

**6**

No, I'm the only one, but I don't mind. The men are funny, and we laugh a lot. I think more women should become firefighters. Women are as brave as men.

**7**

The best thing is knowing that you are doing an important job and saving lives. That makes you feel really good.

**3** Read again and match the questions with the answers. There is one extra question.

a  What does your husband think about the job?

b  So how did you get interested in firefighting?

c  Do you get paid a lot of money?

d  And finally, what's the best thing about the job?

e  What do you like about the job?

f  Did you do any other jobs before you became a firefighter?

g  Are there many women at your fire station?

h  Did you always want to be a firefighter?

**4** Think of three more jobs. Are they usually done by men or women?
What do you think about that?

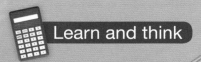 

# Fractions

**1** **Read the ticket and choose the correct answers.**

NEW YORK MUSEUM OF HISTORY

Tues–Sun : 10 a.m.–5 p.m.
Adults $12
Children pay half price

1 How much do adults pay?
   a $4        b $6        c $12

2 What fraction do children pay?
   a ½        b ¼        c ⅓

**2** **Read the sentences and write the fractions.**

   ⅕  ⅓  ¼  ½

1 If we tear the ticket into two pieces, we have two halves. _____

2 If we tear the ticket into three pieces, we have three thirds. _____

3 If we tear the ticket into four pieces, we have four quarters. _____

4 If we tear the ticket into five pieces, we have five fifths. _____

**3** **Look at the pictures. Write the words and then the numbers.**

   tenths   sevenths   ninths   sixths

1 If we tear the ticket into nine pieces, we have nine _____ .

2 If we tear the ticket into six pieces, we have six _____ .

3 If we tear the ticket into ten pieces, we have ten _____ .

4 If we tear the ticket into seven pieces, we have seven _____ .

# Learn and think

## 1 Read and color.

1 two quarters    2 two thirds    3 seven eighths    4 two ninths    5 five tenths

## 2 Think! Look at the coins and discuss in pairs.

1 What do you notice about two quarters and five tenths?

2 What is two eighths the same as?

3 Put the fractions in order of size from biggest to smallest.

> Two quarters and five tenths are …

## 3 Read, write the prices, and answer the questions.

1 Sara had $8 to spend in the museum gift shop. She spent half her money on a teddy bear and a quarter of her money on candy.

How much money did she have left?    $ _____

2 Bobby had $12 to spend in the museum gift shop. He spent a third of his money on a cap and a sixth of his money on a bar of chocolate.

How much money did he have left?    $ _____

3 Who spent the most money?

_____

## 4 Project  My weekend in fractions.

1 Make a pie chart of the activities you will do this weekend.

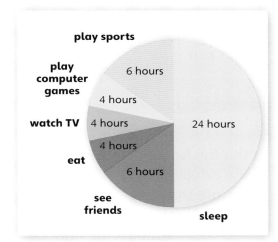

play sports
6 hours
play computer games
4 hours
watch TV  4 hours
24 hours
4 hours
eat
6 hours
see friends
sleep

2 Write the activities as fractions. Remember – there are 48 hours in a weekend.

I spent ½ of my weekend sleeping.

I spent ¹⁄₁₂ of my weekend eating.

I spent ⅛ of my weekend with friends.

## Act it out

# Finding out about an exhibition

**1** **Work in pairs.**
**Choose a role card.**

**Student A**

You want to see an exhibition at a museum.
You are making a phone call to find out about the following:

- if the exhibition is still running
- what the opening times are
- how much the ticket is
- how to get there by public transportation from the train station
- if there is a restaurant there

**Student B**

You work for the museum.
Someone is going to call you to ask you some questions about an exhibition.
Tell them:

- if the exhibition is still running
- about opening times
- about the price of tickets
- if there are long lines
- how to get there from the train station
- if there is a restaurant at the museum

**2** **Act out your dialog.**

## Useful language

**Student A**
Is this the National Museum?
Is the exhibition … ?
What are the … ?
How much are … ?
Could you please tell me how to … ?
Is there a … ?

**Student B**
The exhibition …
We are open from …
The price of …
It might be a good idea to reserve …
There are …
Take bus number …
Yes, we have …

# An advertisement

**1** **Read this advertisement for a robot and answer the questions below.**

Buy ROBOLIX3000 – it'll be your best friend for years because it's the most exciting robot in the universe.

It'll make you happy on sad days, and it'll help you if you are in trouble.

If you're bored, the robot will start playing the drums.

If you're hot, it'll bring you a glass of orange juice.

If you're hungry, it'll make you some sandwiches.

If you want to take a walk and it starts raining, it'll bring an umbrella for you.

If you say, "Good night!" it'll start singing a beautiful song to help you sleep.

**1** Why will Robolix3000 be your best friend for years?

**2** What will it do for you on sad days?

**3** What will it do if you are in trouble?

**4** What will happen if it starts raining?

> Robolix3000 will ...

**Tips for writers**

Before you start writing, think and make notes about your ideas.

**2** **Imagine you are a scientist and are going to build a fancy robot. Write an advertisement for your robot.**

**1** Write down all the things your robot will do to help:

* feel tired – make coffee
* are bored – play the saxophone
* go on vacation – take pictures

**2** Write an advertisement for your robot so lots of people will buy it.

# 9 Mystery at sea

In the 19th century the oceans were full of ships like the one in the picture. People used them for transporting goods around the world. The journeys were often long and very dangerous. Ships spent many months at sea.

1. sail
2. mast
3. captain
4. lifeboat
5. porthole
6. cabin
7. barometer
8. rat
9. sailor

**1** CD4 21 **Listen and say the words. Check with your partner.**

**2** CD4 22 **Read, listen, and complete the sentences.**

1. The ship is much _____ than the *Titanic*.
2. The ship's _____ is standing near the _____ .
3. Phoebe thinks they should _____ for a while.
4. The ship's name is on the wall of the _____ next to the _____ .

**3** **Choose a word. Describe it for your partner to guess.**

You use it to check the weather.

Oh, I know, it's a barometer!

**1** Read Paul's webpage. Check (✓) or put an ✗ in the flags of the places his uncle has visited.

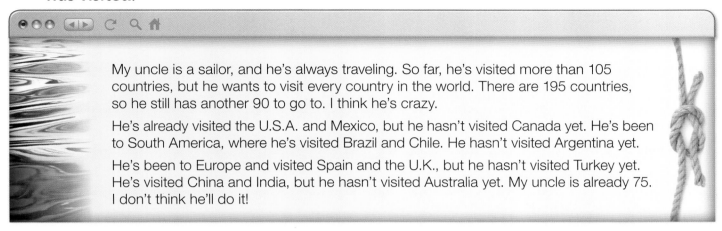

My uncle is a sailor, and he's always traveling. So far, he's visited more than 105 countries, but he wants to visit every country in the world. There are 195 countries, so he still has another 90 to go to. I think he's crazy.

He's already visited the U.S.A. and Mexico, but he hasn't visited Canada yet. He's been to South America, where he's visited Brazil and Chile. He hasn't visited Argentina yet.

He's been to Europe and visited Spain and the U.K., but he hasn't visited Turkey yet. He's visited China and India, but he hasn't visited Australia yet. My uncle is already 75. I don't think he'll do it!

**2** CD 4 • 23   **Grammar focus**   **Listen and say the sentences.**

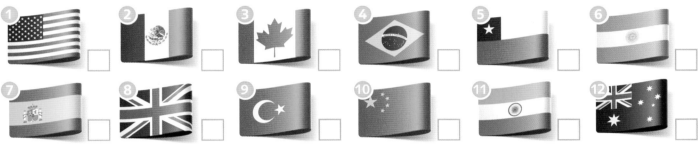

I've **already done** my math homework.
I **haven't done** my English homework **yet**.
My uncle's **already been** to South America.
He **hasn't visited** Argentina **yet**.

**3** Play the coin-tossing game.

I've already done my ...

I haven't done my ...

**1** **CD 4 25** **Listen and write the rhyming words. Then sing the song.**

swim   side   me   sail   ride   see   whale   sea   me   in

Grandma and I one sunny day
Went off for a nice boat (1) _____ ,
When suddenly I turned around,
She wasn't by my (2) _____ .

Captain drop the anchor,
Make your men jump (3) _____ ,
My grandma's fallen in the sea,
I don't think she can (4) _____ !

I ran up to the telescope,
To see what I could (5) _____ .
I rubbed my eyes and looked again
At the beast in front of (6) _____ .

Captain drop the anchor,
Captain drop the (7) _____ ,
My grandma's fallen in the sea,
I think she's in a (8) _____ !

The captain dropped the anchor down,
His men jumped in the (9) _____ .
When suddenly I turned around,
My grandma was next to (10) _____ !

"What's all the fuss about?"

**All about music: Sea Shanties**

Sea shanties were songs that sailors used to sing on their ships many years ago. Their work was often very hard and boring. The sailors were often at sea for many months at a time, and the songs helped the days go faster. Sea shanties are often played on accordions and tin whistles.

**What I think**
▶ It's great.
It's OK.
✖ I don't really like it.

**2** **CD 4 27** **Listen and say the dialog.**

**Cookie** You shouldn't put so much sugar in the pudding, Woody!

**Woody** But look, Cookie. The cookbook says, "Six cupfuls."

**1** CD 4 31 **Listen. Complete the dialogs with the words from the box. Match the dialogs to the pictures.**

parrot   dishes   kitchen   cabin   bath   soup   dinner

**1**

| | |
|---|---|
| **Captain** | Have you finished cleaning my _____ yet? |
| **Sailor** | Well, I've already swept it, but … |
| **Captain** | But what? |
| **Sailor** | … I haven't washed the floor yet. |

**2**

| | |
|---|---|
| **Captain** | Have you finished making _____ yet? |
| **Sailor** | Well, I've already made the _____ , but … |
| **Captain** | But what? |
| **Sailor** | … I haven't made the main course yet. |

**3**

| | |
|---|---|
| **Captain** | Have you finished taking care of my _____ yet? |
| **Sailor** | Well, I've already given him a _____ , but … |
| **Captain** | But what? |
| **Sailor** | … I haven't fed him yet. |

**4**

| | |
|---|---|
| **Captain** | Have you finished cleaning the _____ yet? |
| **Sailor** | Well, I've already done the _____ , but … |
| **Captain** | But what? |
| **Sailor** | … I haven't cleaned the windows yet. |

**2** CD 4 32   **Grammar focus**   **Listen and say the questions and answers.**

**Have** you **cleaned** your bedroom **yet**?
Yes. **I've already done** it.
**Have** you **walked** the dog **yet**?
No. **I haven't done** it **yet**.

**3** **Play the housework game. Find out what your partner has or hasn't done this week.**

- do homework ☐
- walk dog ☐
- clean bedroom ☐
- go shopping ☐
- do dishes ☐
- make breakfast ☐
- feed cat ☐

Have you … yet?

Yes, I have. / No, I haven't.

**1** Go through the text quickly and find answers to the questions.

a    Why were the children hiding?

b    Why did one of the sailors know where the children were hiding?

**2** 🔘 CD4 33 Read and listen to the story to check your answers.

# The *Mary Celeste*

The children hid in a lifeboat and watched the sailors working. They didn't seem very friendly. Two of them came and stood by the lifeboat. "I'm worried," one of them said. "The captain's nervous. He's already shouted at me three times today ... " "Atchoo!" sneezed Patrick. "Oops. I'm sorry!"

The sailors heard the noise and looked in the lifeboat. They found the children and took them to the captain. "Look what we found!" one of them said. "Lock them in my cabin," said the captain. He looked worried. "I'll talk to them later."

The children looked around the cabin. The door would not open. "Now what?" Alex asked. "We'll have to wait and see what the captain says," said Patrick. Phoebe picked up a book from the table. "Hey, listen, guys. It's the captain's diary!" She read aloud, "Things are strange. There is something wrong with this ship. I have a strong feeling that something bad is going to happen ... " "Hurry!" Patrick interrupted. "Come and look out of the porthole!"

"Look at all those lights. It's our gate!" shouted Alex. "We have to go! But those lights are green," said Phoebe. "Our gate's yellow! That's very strange!"

"We have to get out of here," said Patrick. "Let's break the door down." The children picked up the table and banged it against the door. It opened, and they walked out. There were green gates glowing all over the ship. The children were amazed. "Look, there's a sailor. He's walking through one of the green gates!" shouted Alex. The sailor walked through the gate, and a second later he was gone. Everything was silent. There was no one left!

"Now I remember," said Alex. "The *Mary Celeste* was the ship that they found with no one on it. No one knew what happened." "Now we know, but nobody would believe us," said Phoebe. "Look!" shouted Patrick. "There's a yellow light. That's our gate. Come on!" The children stepped into the yellow gate. They were gone in a flash … and landed in their school playground with a thump.

"I don't believe it!" said Phoebe. "We're home. Look, there are Sam and Rob." The Time Travelers ran over to their friends. "Hey, guys!" said Patrick. "You'll never guess what just happened. We had an incredible journey. That explosion in science class created a time tunnel … "

"Very funny! We haven't had science yet. It's this afternoon!" Sam laughed. "Come on, lunch is nearly over, and I want to play soccer." The three friends looked at each other. Were they really back at the right time or was something wrong?

**3** **Match the sentence halves to make the summary.**

| | | | |
|---|---|---|---|
| 1 | The children hide in | a | the captain. |
| 2 | The sailors talk about | b | the table. |
| 3 | The sailors lock the children in | c | green lights. |
| 4 | Phoebe finds a diary on | d | the door. |
| 5 | Patrick looks out of | e | the playground. |
| 6 | The children see lots of | f | the cabin. |
| 7 | The children use the table to break | g | the porthole. |
| 8 | The children arrive in | h | a lifeboat. |

**4** **Think!** **Read and add another answer for each question. Then choose the best answer.**

1 Why was the captain worried?

    a   The ship was going the wrong way.    b   His sailors were all aliens.

    c  _____

2 Where did the sailors go?

    a   into a UFO    b   to another time

    c  _____

3 What might be wrong back at school?

    a   It's not really their school.    b   Their friends don't believe their story.

    c  _____

 **Skills**

### 1 Read the article and match the questions from the box with the answers.

So what's the truth?  Where is it?  What is it?  What has happened there?

# IT'S A WEIRD WORLD: THE BERMUDA TRIANGLE

**1** _____

The Bermuda Triangle is an area in the ocean where many ships and planes have disappeared mysteriously. Nobody can say where they went.

**2** _____

The Bermuda Triangle is in the Atlantic Ocean. The corners of the "triangle" are Miami, Bermuda, and Puerto Rico.

**3** _____

These are two of the famous disappearances:

In 1918, a ship called the *USS Cyclops* disappeared in the area. None of the 306 people on board were ever seen again.

In 1945, a group of fighter planes disappeared while they were flying over the area. The pilots said they could see strange lights in the sky on their radios. The next day another plane went to look for the missing planes. This plane also disappeared.

**4** _____

No one really knows. Some people say that there is nothing mysterious about the area at all. They say that there are a lot of ships in this area, so it's not surprising that sometimes ships go missing. They also say that the bad weather in the area causes a lot of problems.

Other people think the area is more mysterious. Some people believe that aliens take the ships. Other people think that a giant whirlpool pulls ships and planes under the ocean.

What do you think?

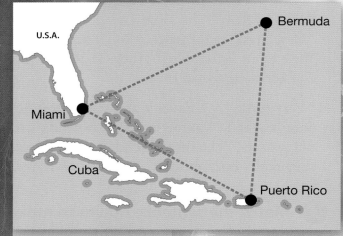

*The Bermuda Triangle*

*Is there a giant whirlpool in the Bermuda Triangle?*

*Planes like these disappeared in 1945.*

### 2 Read again and correct the sentences.

1 The Bermuda Triangle is in the Pacific Ocean.
2 Only ships disappear in the area.
3 The *USS Cyclops* was a plane.
4 In 1945, a plane disappeared in the area.
5 Not many ships sail in the area.
6 The weather is always good in the area.

### 3 Discuss in pairs. What do you think?

I think the Bermuda Triangle is …    That's silly.

Maybe it's …    That's a good idea.

**1** CD4 34 **Listen to the radio show *Mysteries of the Deep* and write the names of the creatures under the pictures.**

mermaids   Loch Ness Monster   Kraken

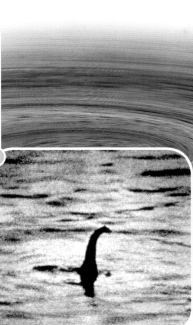

**2** CD4 35 **Listen again and write the names of the creatures next to the sentences.**

1   It pulled ships under the ocean.

2   It doesn't live in the ocean. _____

3   Columbus saw three of them.

4   Everyone wants a picture of this.

5   Was this just a giant octopus?

6   They were friendly. _____

**3** **Draw a picture of a sea monster. Give it a name and write a few sentences about it.**

This is a Trifish. It has three heads and lots of teeth. If you catch a Trifish, it is very bad luck.

# Oceans and seas

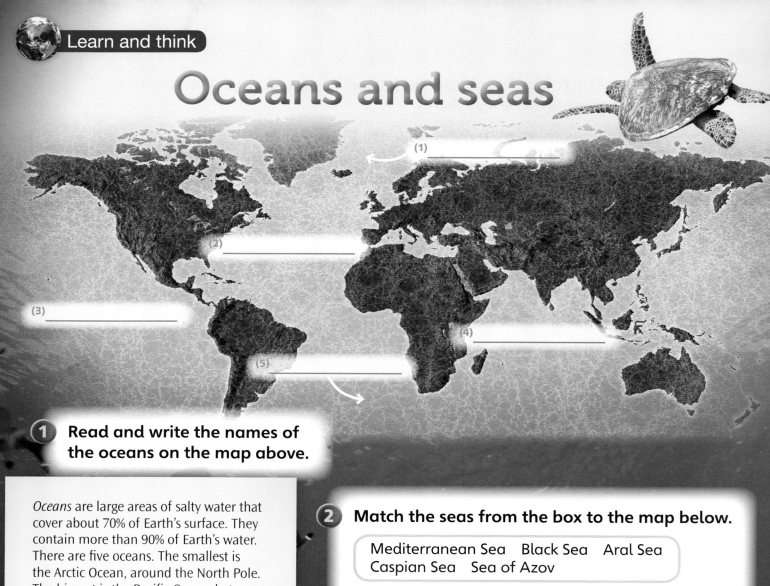

(1) _____
(2) _____
(3) _____
(4) _____
(5) _____

**1** **Read and write the names of the oceans on the map above.**

*Oceans* are large areas of salty water that cover about 70% of Earth's surface. They contain more than 90% of Earth's water. There are five oceans. The smallest is the Arctic Ocean, around the North Pole. The biggest is the Pacific Ocean, between Asia and Australia and North and South America. The Atlantic Ocean lies between west Africa, Europe, and North and South America. The Indian Ocean borders east Africa, south Asia, western Australia, and Antarctica. Finally, there is the Southern Ocean, which is around Antarctica.

We call smaller areas of salty water *seas*. Some seas, like the Caribbean Sea and the North Sea, are part of an ocean. Other seas like the Mediterranean Sea, the Red Sea, and the Black Sea, have small waterways that connect them with an ocean. There are also seas that have no connection with oceans at all, like the Dead Sea, the Caspian Sea, the Sea of Azov, and the Aral Sea.

**2** **Match the seas from the box to the map below.**

Mediterranean Sea   Black Sea   Aral Sea
Caspian Sea   Sea of Azov

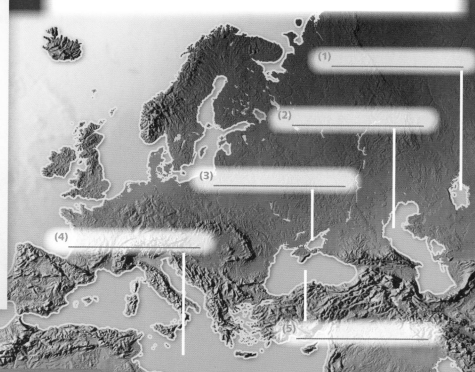

(1) _____
(2) _____
(3) _____
(4) _____
(5) _____

**1** **Think!** **Look and read. Why are seas saltier than rivers?**

evaporation

river (fresh water)

sea/ocean (salt water)

When water flows in rivers, it picks up pieces of salt from the rocks and soil on the riverbeds. These pieces are so small that the river water does not taste salty (we call it fresh water). This water eventually flows into the oceans and seas. Some of the water evaporates in the sun, but the salt does not evaporate. It stays in the ocean. The evaporated water (with no salt in it) then falls as rain into the rivers and starts its trip back to the ocean, again taking tiny bits of salt with it as it goes. Over millions and millions of years, ocean water has become salty because there is more salt in it.

**Smart fact**

The deepest point on Earth is the Mariana Trench in the western Pacific Ocean south of Japan and east of the Philippines. The bottom is 10,924 meters below sea level. Imagine if Mount Everest, at 8,848 meters the highest mountain on Earth, was placed at this location. How many meters under the sea would its top be?

**2** **Project** **Research a river.**

1 Think about these questions and decide which river you want to do your project on.

- Would you like to find out more about a river in your own or another country?
- Look at a map of the country you have chosen. What rivers are there? Which one interests you most?
- Use the Internet or the library to find out more about the river you have chosen.
- How many meters long is it?
- Does it join other rivers / a lake / the ocean?
- What wildlife is in it?
- Does it run through cities? If so, which?
- What shape does it have?

FACTS

- The Thames is 346 kilometers long.
- Its source is close to the village of Kemble, in the Cotswolds.
- Part of the area west of London is sometimes called "the Thames Valley."
- In the 17th and 18th centuries, the Thames often froze in the winter.

The River Thames

2 Write a short text about your river. Use your answers to help you.

3 Draw a map that shows where the river runs. Add the names of cities and other information.

# Small-group talk

**1** CD4 36 Listen to Ruby, Mike, and Sue talking about UFOs. Put these key words in the order you hear them.

☐ little green men

☐ farmer

☐ UFO

☐ scientist

## Find out about it

- Work in groups of three. Choose an unexplained mystery and find out more about it.
- Possible topics are: Bigfoot, the Yeti …
- Use books and magazines.
- Talk to your family and to friends.
- Go online and see what you can find on the Internet.
- In your group, decide what each of you is going to talk about.

## Prepare it

- Each of you tries to find out some important facts about the mystery. Take notes. Compare your notes. Put them in order.
- Find pictures and print them out. Make sure the pictures are big enough for your classmates to see from a distance.
- Decide what each of you is going to say and write your part of the talk. Then show it to your teacher to help you with the language.
- Correct the text if necessary. Read it often enough so that you know what you will say.
- Practice it as a group. Each of you should know when the other one stops so you know when to start. Decide when to show the pictures.

**2** CD4 37 Listen again and answer the questions.

1 What does Ruby talk about?

2 What story does Mike tell?

3 What does Sue say?

> Ruby talks about …

## Present it

- Tell your classmates about your topic and present the pictures.
- You should talk for about a minute, but don't just read your text.
- Make sure that all your classmates can see the pictures.

 **Tips for presenters**

When you practice, check if one of you says "um" or "oh" a lot. If you do, try not to. Your classmates may think that you have not prepared well if there are lots of "ums" and "ohs."

# A summary

**1** **Read the summary of the first four episodes of the Time Travelers and complete with the words from the box. Use each word twice.**

> and   so   but   because

Alex, Phoebe, and Patrick are friends. One day, they have an accident in the school science lab, (1)_____ they create a gateway to different times and places. First, they visit ancient Pompeii. Phoebe sees smoke coming from the volcano and wants to warn the people, (2)_____ the children go to the city. However, the volcano erupts, and it's too late for the people, (3)_____ the children escape when the gateway appears.

Next, the children find themselves in the middle of the jungle. Phoebe thinks they are in South America (4)_____ she can see a jaguar. The children walk through the jungle, (5)_____ they meet some people. Alex gives them a penknife as a present. Then they see the gateway at the top of a waterfall, (6)_____ they climb up it and jump through it.

Next, the children are in 1950s America watching Elvis on stage. After the show, they talk to him. He is afraid to leave (7)_____ there are lots of fans waiting for him. The children think of a plan to help him escape. The children want to stay with Elvis, (8)_____ they know they have to go through the gateway again. They are trying to get home.

**2** **Read the summary of the next three episodes. Write it again and use *and*, *so*, *but*, and *because* to put together the sentence pairs that are marked in color.**

**①** The children are now in the future in a restaurant at the edge of the universe. They find out it is Phoebe's birthday. They decide to celebrate. They have an amazing meal with lots of wonderful food and a birthday cake. The waiter tells them that the meal costs 60,000 goldstars. The children don't have any money. The waiter takes them to the kitchen to do the dishes. They are saved because the gateway appears.

**②** The children arrive in the Wild West. A bank robbery is taking place. They talk to the sheriff. He doesn't do anything. He is scared of the robbers. Alex has a plan. He ties a rope around the robbers' horses' legs. The robbers fall off their horses. The sheriff arrests them. The kids disappear through the gateway.

**③** The next place they arrive in is Istanbul. They decide to go sightseeing, but Phoebe misses the train. She is lost. The boys try to find her. A Turkish boy helps them. Finally, they find Phoebe, and they say goodbye to their new friend as they walk through the gateway to a new adventure.

**3** **Write a summary of the final three episodes of the Time Travelers. Use *and*, *so*, *but*, and *because* to put sentences together.**

**Tips for writers**

When you write a summary, only focus on the most important information. When you have finished, read your text again. Imagine that somebody who has not read the original story is reading it. Would they understand it?

## Grammar focus

# The science class

### Simple past review

> I/He/She **was** at a birthday party.
> It **was** very cold.
> We/You/They **were** at the zoo.
>
> I/You/He/She/It/We/You/They **loved** the food.
> I/You/He/She/It/We/You/They **didn't like** the music.
>
> I/He/She **wasn't** late.
> It **wasn't** sunny.
> We/You/They **weren't** at the party.

**1** **Complete the sentences with the verbs in parentheses.**

1 Yesterday I _____ a lot of work to do. (have)
2 I _____ up very early. (get)
3 I _____ all day. (study)
4 In the evening I _____ my dad in the kitchen. (help)
5 He _____ very happy about that. (be)
6 In the evening I _____ TV. I _____ too tired. (not watch / be)

### Simple past questions review

> **Was** I too loud this morning?
> **Was** he angry?
> **Was** she happy?
> **Were** you at home?
> **Were** they at the stores?
>
> **Did** I **wake** you up?
> **Why did** you **call** me?
> **Did** he **help** you?
> **How did** she **go** to school?
> **Did** it **win**?
> **Did** we **wake** you up?
> **What did** they **say**?

**2** **Choose the correct words.**

1 What did she **study** / **studied**?
2 **Was** / **Were** your sister on vacation?
3 **Was** / **Were** they very hungry?
4 **Did** / **Do** you visit your grandfather yesterday?
5 **How did** / **How do** your test go?
6 Why **was** / **were** you late this morning?

# Disaster!

## Past progressive review

What **were** you **doing** when the fire started?

I **was playing** the guitar
You **were reading** a book
He **was playing** the piano
She **was cooking**
It **was raining**
We/You/They **were dancing** rock 'n' roll

when the fire started.

**1** **Choose the correct words.**

1 I **was** / **were** eating when the phone rang.
2 When the boat arrived, we **was** / **were** buying the tickets.
3 They **was** / **were** cooking when the lights went off.
4 You were sleeping when the movie **started** / **was starting**.
5 When the phone rang, she **worked** / **was working** in the yard.

## Two simultaneous actions with *while*

**While** I **was talking** on the phone,
**While** you **were playing** soccer,
**While** he/she **was repairing** the car,
**While** it **was sunny**,
**While** we **were swimming** in the pool,
**While** they **were having** a barbecue,

the turtle **was eating** the roses.

**2** **Complete the sentences with the verbs in parentheses.**

1 While we were _____ TV, they were lying in the sun. (watch)
2 While he _____ to his neighbor, the dog was barking loudly. (talk)
3 They were playing soccer while their friends _____ to music. (listen)
4 I _____ Dad while you were playing. (help)
5 You were walking the dog while I _____ for my test. (study)

# 2 In the rain forest

## Numbers 100–5,000,000

| | |
|---|---|
| 100 – **one hundred** | 500 – **five hundred** |
| 1,000 – **one thousand** | 5,000 – **five thousand** |
| 10,000 – **ten thousand** | 30,000 – **thirty thousand** |
| 100,000 – **one hundred thousand** | 600,000 – **six hundred thousand** |
| 1,000,000 – **one million** | 2,000,000 – **two million** |

**1** **Write the numbers or the words.**

1  13,000  –  _____

2  _____  –  twelve million

3  4,000  –  _____

4  900,000  –  _____

5  _____  –  seventy thousand

Nine thousand nine hundred ninety-nine!

## *Have to / Had to* review

I/You **have to** eat healthily.
I/You **had to** practice hard.
You **don't have to** do a lot of weightlifting.
**Do** I **have to** smile?

**2** **Make sentences and questions.**

1  to / nine / have / You / bed / go / before / to / .

_____

2  before / get / You / have / don't / to / up / eight / .

_____

3  homework / of / Do / have / do / lot / a / we / to / ?

_____

4  I / Do / to / have / you / call / ?

_____

5  I / to / Do / bring / have / food / any / ?

_____

6  don't / to / You / have / us / come / with / .

_____

# The rock 'n' roll show

## *Going to* review

> I'm **going to** be late!
> **Are** you **going to** play in our team?
> He's **going to** write me an email.
> She's **going to** meet her friends tomorrow.
>
> It's **not going to** rain.
> We're **going to** help you.
> You're **not going to** win the game.
> They're **going to** record a new song.

**1** **Make sentences.**

1 come / not / to / today / They're / school / to / going

_____

2 going / read / to / book / over / this / I'm / the / weekend

_____

3 not / pizza / going / She's / make / to

_____

4 going / They're / Ping-Pong / to / play

_____

5 watch / not / going / the / to / game / We're

_____

## Time: *past* and *to* the hour

It's **twenty past** five.    It's **ten past** twelve.    It's **twenty to** twelve.    It's **ten to** twelve.

**2** **Complete the sentences.**

1 It's _____ .
2 It's _____ .
3 It's _____ .
4 It's _____ .

# 4 Space restaurant

## Ordinal numbers

the **1st (first)** of January
the **2nd (second)** of January
the **3rd (third)** of January
the **4th (fourth)** of January
the **5th (fifth)** of January

**1** Complete the sentences with the dates in parentheses.

1 His birthday's on _the 17th (seventeenth) of May_. (May 17)

2 He's going to leave on _____. (December 1)

3 It's on _____. (January 31)

4 His vacation starts on _____. (February 13)

5 She's arriving on _____. (October 2)

## Zero conditional

**If** you **put** a candle close to the oven, it **melts**.
**If** it **rains**, the grass **gets** wet.
**If** you **stay** in the sun for too long, you **get** sunburned.

**2** Complete the sentences with the verbs in parentheses.

1 If flowers _____ water, they die. (not get)

2 If you heat water to 100 degrees, it _____. (boil)

3 If you put salt on ice, it _____. (melt)

4 If a flame _____ air, it doesn't burn. (not get)

5 If a car _____ of gas, it stops. (run out)

# The Wild West

## Made of ... / Used for ...

This elephant **is made of** glass.
My jeans **are made of** cotton.
This wood's **used for** making furniture.
These books **are used for** teaching French.

**1** **Make sentences.**

1 pencil case / The / made / cotton / of / is

_____

2 are / made / My / leather / of / cow / shoes

_____

3 blankets / for / These / covering / paintings / used / are / the

_____

4 notebooks / are / for / These / drawing / used / pictures

_____

5 used / Gold / is / jewelry / for / making

_____

## Possessive apostrophes

The **pilot's** uniform is dark blue.
The **pilots'** sunglasses look cool.
The **turtle's** shoes are a little too big.
My **sisters'** computers are new.
My **dad's** car is pretty old.
My **parents'** books are in our living room.

**2** **Match the pictures with the sentences. Write numbers.**

1 The girls' jeans are green.
2 The teacher's glasses are red.
3 The boy's jeans are gray.
4 The teachers' glasses are red.
5 The boys' jeans are gray.
6 The girl's jeans are green.

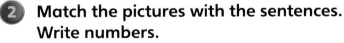

# 6 In Istanbul

## Should/Shouldn't

> You **should** listen carefully to your teacher.
> You **shouldn't** make so much noise in class.

**1** **Choose the correct words.**

1  It's hot. You **should / shouldn't** wear your coat.

2  You have found a golden ring. You **should / shouldn't** report your find.

3  Your little brother has built a sandcastle. You **should / shouldn't** destroy it.

4  There's a great movie at the theater. You **should / shouldn't** come to the movies with us.

5  There are snakes around. You **should / shouldn't** be careful.

## Could I ...? / Do you mind if I ...?

> **Could you** tell me what bus goes to the main square?        Of course.
> **Could I** try on this hat, please?
> **Do you mind if** I look at the cameras?        Not at all.

**2** **Make questions.**

1  me / you / Could / show / way / the / to / stadium / the / ?

_____

2  you / Do / use / mind / I / your / cell / if / phone / ?

_____

3  you / station / tell / where / me / the / is / Could / ?

_____

4  I / talk / Could / for / five / to / minutes / you / ?

_____

5  I / have / tea / Could / cup / another / of / please?

_____

6  you / Do / if / tomorrow / I / come / mind / back / ?

_____

# 7 The story teller

## *Will* for offers and promises

> A  We need some games for the party.    B  I'll **ask** my mom to help us.
> A  It's so cold in here.    B  I'll **shut** the window.
> A  I have a cold.    B  I'll **give** you some medication.

**1**  **Complete the sentences with the verbs in parentheses.**

1  There are no sandwiches left.
   I _____ some more. (make)

2  I'm thirsty.
   I _____ you some orange juice. (get)

3  There's someone at the door.
   I _____ a look. (take)

4  There's been an accident.
   I _____ the police. (call)

5  Peter's still sleeping.
   I _____ him up. (wake)

## Present perfect with *just*

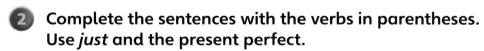

> I've **just spoken** to her. (= have just spoken)
> You've **just broken** my pen. (= have just broken)
> Tom's **just left** for school. (= has just left)
> Karen's **just called**.
> The turtle **has just discovered** a new sport.
> We've **just seen** her.
> They've **just heard** the good news.

**2**  **Complete the sentences with the verbs in parentheses.**
   **Use *just* and the present perfect.**

1  Tom's very happy. He _____ a great present. (get)

2  Ouch! I _____ my knee. (hurt)

3  I'm still tired. I _____ up. (get)

4  Tom and Peter are coming tomorrow! They _____ . (call)

5  Look! I _____ a beautiful feather. (find)

6  We're not hungry. We _____ lunch. (have)

## *If* clauses

> If it **rains**, I'll take my umbrella.
> If you're cold, I'll give you my pullover.
> If they're late, there **won't** be any food for them.

**1** **Complete the sentences with the verbs in parentheses.**

1 If you like fruit, I _____ you some mangos. (get)

2 If you send me an email, I _____ to bring your books. (not forget)

3 If the sun _____ , we'll go swimming. (shine)

4 If you aren't careful, you _____ your leg. (break)

5 If our teacher _____ that, he won't be happy. (hear)

## *What if ... ?*

> **A** Let's go swimming.
> **B** But **what if** it rains?
> **A** Then we'll go home again.
>
> **A** Let's bake a cake for our friends.
> **B** But **what if** it doesn't taste good?
> **A** Then we'll buy one!

**2** **Make sentences and questions.**

1 **A** eat / Let's / apples / these / .

_____

**B** what / are / if / they / not / good / But / ?

_____

**A** we'll / Then / some / eat / bananas / .

_____

2 **A** buy / that / Let's / car / .

_____

**B** if / But / what / it's / expensive / too / ?

_____

**A** Then / buy / a / we'll / motorcycle.

_____

# ⑨ Mystery at sea

## Present perfect with *already* and *yet*

> I've **already been** to New York.
> You've **already told** me that.
> He's **already had** lunch.
> She's **already heard** this song.
>
> It's **already been** eaten.
> We've **already tried** this food.
> They've **already been** here.
>
> I/You/We/They **haven't seen** this **yet**.
> He/She **hasn't done** her homework **yet**.

**1** **Make sentences.**

1   hasn't / She / to / London / been / yet

_____

2   already / the / They've / money / found

_____

3   told / I / you / haven't / yet

_____

4   already / all / read / the / We've / books

_____

5   yet / haven't / shopping / gone / You

_____

## *Have you ... yet?*

> **A** **Have** you **called** your brother **yet**?
> **B** Yes, I've **already** done it.
>
> **A** **Have** you **called** your sister **yet**?
> **B** No, I **haven't done** it **yet**.
>
> **A** **Have** you **cooked** the spaghetti **yet**?
> **B** Yes, I've **already** done it.

**2** **Complete the sentences with the verbs in parentheses.**

1   **A** Have you _____ your bike yet? (clean)
    **B** Yes, _____ .

2   **A** Have you _____ your dinner yet? (eat)
    **B** No, _____ .

3   **A** Have you _____ your homework yet? (do)
    **B** Yes, _____ .

4   **A:** Have you _____ the cat yet? (feed)
    **B** No, _____ .

# Thanks and acknowledgments

## Authors' thanks

We would like to thank our editorial team very warmly: Aldona Gawlinski and Bridget Kelly. You have worked extremely hard and with a lot of dedication to make this course a success. It was a pleasure working with you on this project. Thank you for your commitment, and for your great sense of humor!

We would also like to thank Maria Pylas, Regional Publishing Director, for many interesting discussions and for choosing us as the author team for this project. It's been a great experience, Maria!

## The publishers are grateful to the following contributors:

Oliver Design: concept desig
Blooberry Design: cover des    book design, and page make-up
Hilary Fletcher: picture rese
John Marshall Media Inc.: au    cordings
Tim Woolf: song writing
Karen Elliott: phonics author
Lisa Hutchins: freelance editor
hyphen S.A.: publishing management, American English edition

Special thanks to Kay Bentley and Robert Quinn for their contribution in the development of the "English for school" sections of the Student's Book.

Special thanks to Karen Elliott for developing and writing the phonics material.

## The publishers and authors would like to thank the following teachers and reviewers for their help in developing the course:

**Argentina:** Paula Coudannes, Liliana Amado, María Silvia Caride, Gabriela Finkelstein, Susana Lagier, Gladys Ledwith, María Sol Luppi, Mónica Marinakis, Silvia Miranda, Natalia Monty, Pamela Pogré, Adriana Raffo, Viviana Rondina, Inés Salomón, Stella Maris Schulte, María Teresa de Vido de Stringa, María Marta Taurozzi

**Chile:** Sandra Durán Vega, Fernanda Tornero

**Egypt:** Nabil Ezz-el Deen, Iglal El Gamel, Ghada Farouk, Nemat Matta, Sonia Abdul Rahman, Daniel Rolph, Amy Sarkiss

**Mexico:** Claudia Mejía Escalante, Lucia García, Imelda Calderón Gómez, Laura Landa Herrera, Yeymi Ortiz Iberra, Claudia Camacho Jiménez, Rosa María Martínez Maldonado, José Antonio Martínez, Guadalupe Mejía, María Teresa Moguel, María del Rosario Limón Ortiz, María Teresa Patrón, Yara Gil Pérez, Lorena Sánchez Pérez, Ivette Portales, Yolanda Gómez Saldana, Diana Naim Sucar

**Poland:** Ewa Orłowska-Przezdziecka

**Portugal:** Niki Joseph

**Qatar:** Eilidh Hamilton

**Spain:** Arantxa Abalos, Julius Krajewski, Ángela McClenaghan, Ken O'Carroll, Noreen O'Donnell, John West, Valerie Weston

**Turkey:** Deniz Altiparmak, Lisa Broomhead, Celia Gasgil

**U.K.:** Lucy Frino, Pippa Mayfield, Susannah Reed, Hilary Ratcliff, Melanie Williams

## The publishers are grateful to the following illustrators:

Maurizio de Angelis (Beehive Illustration), Galia Bernstein (NB Illustration), Robin Boyden (Pickled Ink), Sam Church (Organise Art), Christian Cornia (Advocate Art), Daniela Dogliano (Bright Agency), Peter Dobbin (Pickled Ink), Mark Duffin, Anna Hymas (New Division), Colin Howard (Advocate Art), Graham Kennedy, Kate Rochester (Pickled Ink), Alan Rowe, Simon Rumble (Beehive Illustration), Rupert Van Wyk (Beehive Illustration), Dirty Vectors,

The authors and publishers acknowledge the following sources of copyright material and are grateful for the permissions granted. While every effort has been made, it has not always been possible to identify the sources of all the material used, or to trace all copyright holders. If any omissions are brought to our notice, we will be happy to include the appropriate acknowledgements on reprinting.

T = Top, C = Center, B = Below, L = Left, R = Right, B/G = background

p. 11 (T): Alamy/© PSL Images; p. 12 (B/G tartan): Shutterstock.com/NemesisINC; p. 12 (B/G gray): Shutterstock.com/Daniiel; p. 12 (belt): Thinkstock/PhotoObjects.net; p. 12 (boots): Thinkstock/iStockphoto; p. 12 (punk): Thinkstock/Photodisc; p. 12 (closed safety pins): Thinkstock/iStockphoto; p. 12 (open safety pin): Shutterstock.com/Swapan Photography; p. 12 (CL): Thinkstock/iStockphoto; p. 12 (BR): Corbis/© Mike Laye; p. 16 (Skills icon): Shutterstock.com/rvlsoft; p. 16 (B/G): Thinkstock/iStockphoto; p. 16 (TL): Shutterstock.com/warmer; p. 16 (TCL): Getty Images/AFP/Ronaldo Schemidt; p. 16 (TR): Evgeny Dubinchuk/Shutterstock.com; p. 16 (BR): Getty Images/Science Faction/Ed Darack; p. 17 (Skills icon): Shutterstock.com/Bedrin; p. 17 (L): Rex Features; p. 17 (R): Rex Features/Sipa Press; p. 18 (Learn and think icon): Shutterstock.com/Alex Staroseltsev; p. 18 (B/G R): Thinkstock/Hemera; p. 18 (L): Shutterstock.com/Asaf Eliason; p. 18 (C): Alamy/© Greg Vaughn; p. 18 (R): Shutterstock.com/LilKar; p. 18-19 (B/G): Thinkstock/Hemera; p. 19 (Learn and think icon): Shutterstock.com/Alex Staroseltsev; p. 19 (B/G B): Thinkstock/iStockphoto; p. 20 (Time to present icon): Shutterstock.com/Camilo Torres; p. 20 (TL): Thinkstock/iStockphoto; p. 20 (TR): Getty Images/Flickr/Willoughby Owen; p. 20 (B): Press Association Images/AP Photo/Mark Schiefelbein; p. 21 (My portfolio icon): Shutterstock.com/ra2studio; p. 21 (C): Corbis/© Randy Faris; p. 23 (TL): Thinkstock/iStockphoto; p. 23 (TR): Thinkstock/Hemera; p. 24 (Communication icon): Shutterstock.com/Palto; p. 25 (L, CL, C, R): Thinkstock/iStockphoto; p. 28 (Skills icon): Shutterstock.com/Bedrin; p. 28 (TL): Rex Features/Mike Maloney; p. 28 (TR): Thinkstock/neelsky; p. 28 (B): Getty Images/Lonely Planet Images/Amos Chapple; p. 29 (Skills): Shutterstock.com/rvlsoft; p. 29: Press Association Images/AP/Gleison Miranda; p. 30 (Learn and think icon): Shutterstock/Hal_P; p. 30 (B/G fern): Shutterstock.com/apdesign; p. 30 (B/G

butterfly): Thinkstock/Hemera; p. 30 (TL): Rex Features/Sutton-Hibbert; p. 30 (CR): Corbis/© Kazuyoshi Nomachi; p. 30 (BR): Alamy/© ImageState; p. 30-31 (B/G jungle): Thinkstock/iStockphoto; p. 31 (Learn and think icon): Shutterstock/Hal_P; p. 31 (BR): Thinkstock/iStockphoto; p. 32 (Act it out): Thinkstock/iStockphoto; p. 33 (My portfolio icon): Shutterstock.com/ra2studio; p. 36 (B/G BL): Thinkstock/iStockphoto; p. 36 (B/G TL): Thinkstock/iStockphoto; p. 36 (B/G BR): Thinkstock/Hemera; p. 36 (TL): Thinkstock/iStockphoto; p. 36 (TC): Thinkstock/iStockphoto; p. 36 (TR): Thinkstock/Brand X Pictures; p. 36 (CL): Getty Images/Michael Ochs Archives; p. 36 (C): Thinkstock/PhotoObjects.net; p. 36 (CR): Thinkstock/iStockphoto; p. 37 (TL): Shutterstock.com/spaxiax; p. 37 (TC): Thinkstock/iStockphoto; p. 37 (TR): Thinkstock/Brand X Pictures; p. 37 (CL): Alamy/© Sean Gladwell; p. 37 (CR): Shutterstock.com/ zhekoss; p. 39: Thinkstock/iStockphoto; p. 40 (Skills icon): Shutterstock.com/Bedrin; p. 40 (B/G): Thinkstock/iStockphoto; p. 40 (T): Alamy/© Tanguy LeNeel; p. 40 (BL): Getty Images/The Image Bank.Peter Hince; p. 40 (BR): Thinkstock/iStockphoto; p. 41 (Skills icon): Shutterstock.com/rvlsoft; p. 42 (Learn and think icon): Shutterstock.com/koya979; p. 42 (B/G T): Thinkstock/Hemera; p. 42 (B/G C): Thinkstock/Photodisc; p. 42 (TR): Getty Images/DEX IMAGE; p. 42 (CL): Shutterstock.com/Eduard Kyslynskyy; p. 42 (C): Thinkstock/PhotoObjects.net; p. 43 (Learn and think icon): Shutterstock.com/koya979; p. 43 (B/G TR): Thinkstock/Ingram Publishing; p. 44 (Time to present icon): Shutterstock.com/Camilo Torres; p. 45 (My portfolio icon): Shutterstock.com/ra2studio; p. 47 (TR): Shutterstock.com/Goodluz; p. 47 (B): Thinkstock/Hemera; p. 48 (Communication icon): Shutterstock.com/Palto; p. 52 (Skills icon): Shutterstock.com/rvlsoft; p. 52 (B/G): Thinkstock/iStockphoto; p. 52: CHARLIE AND THE CHOCOLATE FACTORY by Roald Dahl (Puffin Books, 2007). Text Copyright © Roald Dahl Nominee Ltd, 1964 Illustrations Copyright © Quentin Blake, 1995; p. 53 (Skills icon): Shutterstock.com/Bedrin; p. 53 (Ex1 CR): Thinkstock/iStockphoto; p. 54 (Learn and think icon): Shutterstock.com/Sashkin; p. 54 (B/G banana, strawberry, orange, pineapple): Thinkstock/iStockphoto; p. 54 (boy jumping): Shutterstock.com/Eduard Stelmakh; p. 54 (boy eating): Thinkstock/F1online; p. 54-55 (B/G): Shutterstock.com/Evlakhov Valeriy; p. 54-55 (B/G C): Thinkstock/Hemera; p. 54-55 B/G CT): Thinkstock/iStockphoto; p. 55 (Learn and think icon): Shutterstock.com/Sashkin; p. 55 (B/G TR): Thinkstock/Stockbyte; p. 55 (B/G CR): Thinkstock/Comstock; p. 55 (B/G BL): Thinkstock/iStockphoto; p. 55 (B/G pen): Thinkstock/PhotoObjects.net; p. 55 (mango): Shutterstock.com/Maks Narodenko; p. 55 (onions): Shutterstock.com/ Petr Malyshev; p. 55 (meat): Getty Images/FoodPix/Carin Krasner; p. 55 (wheat): Shutterstock.com/illustrart; p. 55 (cream): Getty Images/Photolibrary/Maximilian Stock Ltd.; p. 56 (Act it out icon): Thinkstock/iStockphoto; p. 57 (My portfolio icon): Shutterstock.com/ra2studio; p. 59 (Ex3 pencil): Alamy/© Ingvar Björk; p. 59 (Ex3 pen): Shutterstock.com/Aleksandr Bryliaev; p. 59 (Ex3 glass): Shutterstock.com/haveseen; p. 59 (Ex3 bottle): Shutterstock.com/design56; p. 59 (Ex3 guitar): Shutterstock.com/Africa Studio; p. 59 (Ex3 trumpet): Shutterstock.com/magicoven; p. 59 (Ex3 hat): Shutterstock.com/TerraceStudio; p. 59 (Ex3 scarf): Shutterstock.com/iStockphoto; p. 59 (EX3 shoes): Thinkstock/iStockphoto; p. 59 (Ex3 knife and fork): Thinkstock/iStockphoto; p. 60 (B/G wood planks): Thinkstock/iStockphoto; p. 60 (B/G landscape): Thinkstock/Comstock; p. 60 (TR): Thinkstock/Hemera; p. 60 (CL): Thinkstock/iStockphoto; p. 60 (C): Thinkstock/iStockphoto; p. 60 (BL): Thinkstock/Brand X Pictures; p. 60 (BR): Getty Images/Vetta/Renee Keith; p. 64 (Skills icon): Shutterstock.com/rvlsoft; p. 64 (TL): Getty Images/Image Source; p. 64 (TR): Shutterstock.com/KUCO; p. 64 (BL): Shutterstock.com/Jim Parkin; p. 65 (Skills icon): Shutterstock.com/Bedrin; p. 66 (Learn and think icon): Shutterstock.com/Alex Staroseltsev; p. 66 (B/G T): Thinkstock/Photos.com; p. 66 (L): Thinkstock/iStockphoto; p. 66 (L): Corbis/Reuters/© Mike Hutchings; p. 66 (R): Superstock/Robert Harding Picture Library; p. 66-67 (B/G C): Thinkstock/iStockphoto; p. 67 (Learn and think icon): Shutterstock.com/Alex Staroseltsev; p. 67 (B/G TR): Thinkstock/Comstock; p. 67 (B): Thinkstock/Photodisc; p. 67 (TL): Alamy/©allOver photography; p. 67 (CL): Getty Images/DAJ; p. 67 (BL): Thinkstock/iStockphoto; p. 68 (Time to present icon): Shutterstock.com/Camilo Torres; p. 69 (My portfolio icon): Shutterstock.com/ra2studio; p. 72 (Communication icon): Shutterstock.com/Palto; p. 76 (Skills icon): Shutterstock.com/rvlsoft; p. 76 (B): Thinkstock/Photodisc; p. 76 (flags): Shutterstock.com/Alhovik; p. 76 (B): Alamy/© Nina Kissell; p. 77 (Skills icon): Shutterstock.com/Bedrin; p. 78 (Learn and think icon): Shutterstock.com/Alex Staroseltsev; p. 78-79 (B/G T): Thinkstock/iStockphoto; p. 78 (B/G CL): Thinkstock/Comstock; p. 78-79 (B/G B): Thinkstock/iStockphoto; p. 78-79 (B/G BC): Thinkstock/iStockphoto; p. 78 (T): Alamy/© Cultura Creative; p. 78 (waitress, chef, doctor): Thinkstock/iStockphoto; p. 78 (nurse): Thinkstock/BananaStock; p. 78 (train driver): Superstock/Marka; p. 78 (buying a ticket): Getty Images/Taxi/Erik Dreyer; p. 78 (supermarket): Thinkstock/iStockphoto; p. 78 (teacher): Thinkstock/iStockphoto; p. 78 (coach): Thinkstock/Brand X Pictures; p. 79 (Learn and think icon): Shutterstock.com/Alex Staroseltsev; p. 79 (L): Thinkstock/Creatas; p. 79 (CL): Getty Images/The Image Bank/Ron Levine; p. 79 (CR): Thinkstock/Monkey Business; p. 79 (R): Thinkstock/iStockphoto; p. 79 (B/G BR): Thinkstock/iStockphoto; p. 80 (Act it out icon): Thinkstock/iStockphoto; p. 81 (My portfoilio icon): Shutterstock.com/ra2studio; p. 81 (L): Thinkstock/iStockphoto; p. 81 (R): Getty Images/Taxi/Chris Clinton; p. 84 (B/G L): Thinkstock/iStockphoto; p. 84 (B/G TL): Thinkstock/iStockphoto; p. 84 (B/G R): Thinkstock/iStockphoto; p. 84 (B/G CR): Thinkstock/Comstock; p. 84 (B/G BR): Thinkstock/iStockphoto; p. 84 (BC):Getty Images/WireImage/James Devaney; p. 84 (BC): Getty Images/Redferns/GAB Archive; p. 88 (Skills icon): Shutterstock.com/Bedrin; p. 88 (L): Front cover to be used in its entirety of GRIMMS FAIRY TALES by Jacob and Wilhelm Grimm (Penguin Books, 2010); p. 88 (CL): Front cover to be used in its entirety of THE VERY HUNGRY CATERPILLAR by Eric Carle (Puffin Books, 1994). Illustrations copyright G Eric Carle, 1969 and 1987; p. 88 (CR): Cover of Birds of America by JJ Audubon, published by Natural History Museum reproduced with permission; p. 88 (R): Cover of Gadsby by E V Wright, published by Ramble House with a dust jacket created by Gavin L. O'Keefe reproduced with permission. www.ramblehouse.com; p. 89 (Skills): Shutterstock.com/rvlsoft; p. 89 (book): Thinkstock/iStockphoto; p. 90 (Skills icon): Shutterstock.com/Natalia Siverina; p. 90 (TC): Thinkstock/iStockphoto; p. 90-91 (B/G): Thinkstock/Hemera; p. 91 (Skills icon): Shutterstock.com/Natalia Siverina; p. 91 (B/G BR): Thinkstock/iStockphoto; p. 91 (CL): Thinkstock/iStockphoto; p. 91 (CR): Thinkstock/iStockphoto; p. 92 (Time to present icon): Shutterstock.com/Camilo Torres; p. 93 (My portfolio icon): Shutterstock.com/ra2studio; p. 93 (BL): Alamy/© FALKENSTEINFOTO; p. 93 (BC): Thinkstock/Fuse; p. 96 (Communication icon): Shutterstock.com/Palto; p. 100 (Skills icon): Shutterstock.com/Bedrin; p. 101 (Skills icon): Shutterstock.com/rvlsoft; p. 101 (R): Thinkstock/Hemera; p. 102 (Learn and think icon): Shutterstock.com/Mile Atanasovl; p. 102-103 (B/G): Thinkstock/Photodisc; p. 103 (Learn and think icon): Shutterstock.com/Mile Atanasov; p. 103 (TL): Thinkstock/iStockphoto; p. 103 (TR): Thinkstock/Stockbyte; p. 103 (BL): Shutterstock.com/Coprid; p. 103 (BR): Thinkstock/Hemera; p. 104 (Act it out icon): Thinkstock/iStockphoto; p. 105 (My portfolio icon): Shutterstock.com/ra2studio; p. 107 (TL): Thinkstock/Comstock; p. 107 (TR):Thinkstock/Hemera; p. 107 (1, 2, 3, 6, 7, 9, 10, 11): Shutterstock.com/Alhovik; p. 107 (4, 5, 8, 12): iStockphoto/pialhovik; p. 108 (B/G L): Thinkstock/iStockphoto; p. 108 (B/G R): Thinkstock/iStockphoto; p. 108 (TC): Thinkstock/Stockbyte; p. 108 (C): Thinkstock/Photos.com; p. 108 (wheel): Thinkstock/PhotoObjects.net; p. 108 (anchor): Thinkstock/Hemera; p. 112 (Skills icon): Shutterstock.com/rvlsoft; p. 112 (B/G): Getty Images/Flickr Open/delreycarlos; p. 112 (BR): Rex Features/ITV; p. 113 (Skills icon): Shutterstock.com/Bedrin; p. 113 (B/G): Getty Images/Flickr Open/delreycarlos; p. 113 (1): Alamy/© North Wind Picture Archives; p. 113 (3): Corbis/© Cynthia Hart Designer; p. 113 (2): Alamy/© AF archive; p. 114 (Learn and think icon): Shutterstock.com/Alex Staroseltsev; p. 114 (B/G): Thinkstock/Hemera; p. 114 (TR): Thinkstock/iStockphoto; p. 115 (Learn and think icon): Shutterstock.com/Alex Staroseltsev; p. 115 (BR): Thinkstock/iStockphoto; p. 116 (Time to present icon): Shutterstock.com/Camilo Torres; p. 116 (TL): Corbis/©Bettmann; p. 116 (TR): Getty Images/The Image Bank.Steven Peters; p. 116 (B): Getty Images/Hulton Archive/Barney Wayne; p. 117 (My portfolio icon): Shutterstock.com/ra2studio.

Commissioned photography by: Gareth Boden p. 5, 7, 11 (B), 13, 19 (L, R), 23 (B), 25 (CR), 32 (BR), 35, 37 (B), 42, 48, 49, 53 (Ex1 L, CL, C, CR, TR, Ex2), 56 (B), 67 (R), 71, 73, 80 (B), 85, 95, 104 (B). Neil Matthews at Phaebus p. 24, 48a and b, 72, 96.

HarperCollins Publishers for the poem on p. 90 'My mother makes me chicken' from A Pizza the size of the Sun, text copyright © 1996 by Jack Prelutsky, published by Greenwillow Books. Reproduced with permission; United Agents for the poem on p. 90 'Fame' by Roger McGough from Nailing the Shadow, copyright © Roger McGough, 1987. Reproduced by permission of United Agents (www.unitedagents.co.uk) on behalf of Roger McGough; HarperCollins Children's Books and Edite Kroll Literary Agency Inc for the poem and illustration on p. 90 'Spaghetti' from Where the Sidewalk Ends by Shel Silverstein, published by Harper and Row. Copyright © 1974, renewed 2002 Evil Eye Music, LLC. Reprinted with permission from the Estate of Shel Silverstein, HarperCollins Children's Books and Edite Kroll Literary Agency Inc; David Higham Associates for the text on pp. 52–53 adapted from the magazine The Magical World of Roald Dahl: Charlie and the Chocolate Factory by Roald Dahl, Puffin Books 2006. Reproduced with permission;

Marathon Music International for the sound-alike recording of Don't be cruel, licensed from Marathon Music International.